How To
Incorporate
Your
Texas
Business

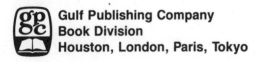

Gulf Publishing Company
Book Division
Houston, London, Paris, Tokyo

How To
Incorporate
Your
Texas
Business

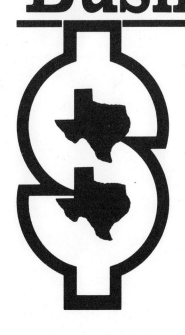

Tom Branton

To my parents, Mr. and Mrs. Milton F. Branton

How to Incorporate Your Texas Business

Library of Congress Cataloging in Publication Data

Branton, Thomas M.
How to incorporate your Texas business.

Bibliography: p.
Includes index.
1. Corporation law—Texas. 2. Incorporation—Texas.
I. Title.
KFT1413.B65 1984   346.764′066   83-22634
ISBN 0-87201-423-1   347.640666

Acknowledgments

Even the writing of a simple book requires the assistance of many people. I'd like to thank Professor Charles Ferguson of the English Department of Alvin Community College for his review of the manuscript, and his many suggestions for conveying thoughts in a nonlegalese manner. Thanks also go to my other colleagues at Alvin Community College for their support and encouragement.

I am certainly grateful to a number of attorneys for their comments and suggestions, especially my law partner, William R. Bitner, and my wife, Mary K. Branton.

My thanks to my typist Mary Henry and my legal secretary Elizabeth Finger for their assistance.

My thanks also to West Publishing Company for their permission to reproduce statutes from their copyrighted version of the Texas Business Corporation Act, the Office of the Secretary of State for permission to reproduce materials from their *Filing Guide for Corporations and Limited Partnerships,* and to Tim Calk of Gulf Publishing Company for his suggestions and ideas.

Special thanks to my clients: Thank you for your thoughtful questions and the ideas you have given me to think upon. I have learned much from you as I hope you have learned from me.

I would certainly appreciate any suggestions or comments a reader of this book may have.

Contents

of Directors Meeting 61, Meetings of Shareholders 62, Summary 66.

Preface

I wrote this book as an easy-to-read and understandable guide to the process and aftermath of incorporating a Texas business. For years, my clients have asked me for a simple explanation of the incorporation process, its benefits and disadvantages. My first thought was that there must be a well written book available, but after a diligent search I could find nothing relevant to Texas law and of a caliber that I would recommend to my clients. Therefore, this book came into being.

At some point in the life of a business, perhaps at the beginning or perhaps later, you as the owner of that business will face an important decision. Should you incorporate? The libraries of our cities and schools are well supplied with technical and legal works on corporations, but most are written for attorneys and students of the law rather than business persons. This book is for you, the owner of a new or existing business who is interested in the corporate form of business. Written in practical terms, it will help you make an informed, intelligent decision on incorporation, and will additionally provide you with an understanding of the advantages of incorporation, the process of incorporation, and the operation of a business as a corporation.

While writing this book, I always tried to keep in mind to whom this information is directed. Rather than being a legal encyclopedia on corporations, this is a handbook for the business owner. So, in some instances, the information and procedures have been generalized and simplified in order to convey a principle or thought. In addition to giving you a basic understanding of the Texas corporation, it will make your transition into such a business form easier, more knowledgeable, and more profitable. Good luck and may you prosper.

Tom Branton
Friendswood, Texas

Chapter 1

Should You Incorporate?

Most businesses with owners who are thinking of incorporating fall into two distinct categories—the *existing business* and the *new business*.

Imagine you have been in business for several years and now have what you consider to be a successful venture. Like most business owners, you have concerns about the economy, interest rates, expansion, and your future. However, perhaps two of your greatest concerns are legal liability, if you should be sued, and taxes. Other business people in your town have incorporated and have told you that they pay less taxes and are protected in case they are sued. You are interested in becoming a corporation.

On the other hand, there is this scenario. It has finally happened. After several years of saving enough money and finding the right location, you have established a new business in town. Perhaps you look with some envy at the already existing businesses in town and their established reputation and customers, but you have the drive and determination to make it. However, there are some things you are concerned about. You know the established businesses are incorporated. What do they know that you do not? At what point will your new business grow into one that should be incorporated? You are interested in knowing about becoming a corporation.

What Is a Corporation?

The best way to explain a corporation is to compare it with two other forms of business. First, let us consider the sole proprietorship. This form is a one-person business. Legally you are the business, and it is you. You will notice that legal documents refer to your business as, for example, "Fred Duke, doing business as Duke's Interiors." A partnership is not a great deal different except that you have two or more individuals owning a business together. An example of such a business is "Dukes' Interiors, a partnership composed of Fred Duke and John Duke." In this case you both are the business, and it is you.

A corporation is a different situation entirely. In a corporation the business exists as a separate legal entity. This entity is given life by a charter granted by the secretary of state of Texas. It is much like a separate person apart from you. Your ownership of the business may be reflected by a stock certificate, but the business itself is not a part of you individually. This one unique characteristic is the basis for some of the best advantages of incorporating your business.

Initial Investigation of the Corporation

Let us say that you, the new or seasoned business owner, have an appointment with your attorney to discuss an incorporation. You are expecting to have explained to you, in a clear and definite manner, the factors and benefits to be gained from incorporation. You want to know the advantages and the problems, and to have a sound basis upon which to make the decision to incorporate. Unfortunately, you may be somewhat disappointed by the information given you, and a plain fact must be recognized: not all attorneys are created equal. Those without a business and accounting background sometimes cannot give you a good explanation of the factors relating to incorporation, because they truly do not understand those factors themselves. Most of these attorneys either do not have contact with corporate clients or pass them on to a well-informed associate. (See Chapter 2 for a more detailed explanation of how to seek the right attorney to incorporate your business.) It is hoped that the correct attorney will, with you as his guide, analyze your business according to the following factors:

1. Considering the nature of your business, what is the possibility of a lawsuit against you?
2. Are you presently operating your business at a profit or loss? What is your future outlook?
3. Does the nature of your business allow it to be conducted as a corporation, and are you willing to do so?
4. How many people are to be involved in the business as owners and/or employees, and what is the relationship between them?
5. What fringe benefits do you as the owner desire?
6. What is your tax position in the business?
7. How will the business be financed?
8. Do any other factors exist that will have a bearing upon the incorporation of the business?

At the end of the discussion, the attorney should have the data needed to give you a good recommendation on incorporation. Be skeptical of the attorney who does not take the time to help you evaluate your business and quickly starts you down the incorporation road with a telephone call. In such an instance you will probably be without trustworthy guidance throughout the entire procedure.

Advantages of Incorporation

First, the corporation is not a cure-all. It is not a miracle form of business that will positively make you rich, protect you from all taxes, guarantee you a life of luxury, and secure your carefree retirement in the Hill Country. Many business proprietors will hear a great deal of misinformation about the benefits of incorporation. Some of this misinformation comes from clients of attorneys who have misunderstood some benefit. (One purpose of this book is to help you to understand your attorney.) Other problems result from writers in the field who promote the corporation as a remedy for all business problems and a way to quick riches. Those writers are the only ones who get rich.

Second, even though it is not the absolute cure-all, there are some real advantages to certain businesses operating as corporations. These advantages can be divided into tax and non-tax categories.

Tax Advantages

☐ *Qualified Retirement Plans.* Although recent federal legislation has somewhat equalized retirement plans between corporations and other forms of business, the fact remains that if a business generates cash in excess of the owner's personal needs, this excess cash may be placed in a retirement plan and not be taxed, either on the initial investment or the interest earned, until the cash is withdrawn from the plan. In addition, the corporation may use its contribution to the retirement plan as a tax deduction.

☐ *Health, Medical and Disability Insurance.* The company may provide for its employees' health, medical, and/or disability insurance plans, the cost of which is a deduction to the corporation and not considered as income of the employee-owner.

☐ *Medical Reimbursement Plans.* The corporation may agree to pay all medical expenses not covered by the above plans, such as the deductible amounts. This cost is also a deduction to the corporation and is not taxable to the person receiving the reimbursement. In many cases, this type plan is used in the small family corporation to cover medical expenses that cannot be insured or may be too expensive to cover, such as dental and vision-correction expenses.

☐ *Term Life Insurance.* Group term life insurance may be provided for employees in amounts up to $50,000.00. The premiums are deductible by the corporation and not considered as employee income.

☐ *Corporate Tax Rates.* These tax rates are a great deal lower than personal individual rates. The 1984 tax rates are as follows:

First $25,000.00 of income	15%
Next $25,000.00 of income	18%
Next $25,000.00 of income	30%
Next $25,000.00 of income	40%
All income greater than $100,000.00	46%

This advantage is most useful to the corporation when monies must be accumulated to make large capital purchases. In sole proprietorships and partnerships, money used for capital purchases will already have been taxed at whatever personal tax rate the owners are in. Corporations making capital purchases may use monies only taxed at the above rate.

☐ *Business Expenses.* Although in theory there should be no great difference between the deductibility of expenses for sole proprietorships and partnerships on the one hand and corporations on the other, many accountants feel more comfortable placing these expenses on a corporate tax return. This practice also keeps your personal return free of numerous deductions.

Non-Tax Advantages

☐ *Form of Business.* A corporation is a much more formal and structured form of business. Often the fact that owners have to keep better records, hold corporate meetings, make decisions by majority rule, and follow the normal corporate procedures makes them more businesslike in everyday management activities.

☐ *Transferability of Vested Interest.* Since ownership of the corporation is reflected by stock, you can transfer any percentage of the stock to whatever party you wish to have a vested interest in the corporation. These may be employees, family members, new investors, or whomever you desire. This is an excellent method of gradually bringing trusted employees or family members into the business.

In a partnership, if you are concerned about the consequences of the death of one of the owners and the effect it will have on the business, you may decide to incorporate. Since the corporation is a separate legal entity apart from the owner-stockholders, the death of one of them will not affect the continued legal existence of the business. Through a buy-out agreement you can plan that in the event of a shareholder's death, the corporation will purchase that person's stock from his or her heirs at a price established before that shareholder's death. Many corporations buy life insurance on stockholders' lives to fund these agreements.

☐ *Limited Liability.* As a general rule, the owner of a properly formed and operated corporation does not stand to lose any more than his or her investment in the business in the event the business is sued and loses the case. Aside from some tax benefits, this is probably the most important advantage to an incorporated business. It means that the personal assets of the owner are not subject to the suit and cannot be taken in the event of loss. Only what is owned by the corporation is subject to the suit. There are few absolutely safe business ventures in this world. Although most owners keep themselves and their employees adequately insured against injury to customers and faulty work, a corporation may be the only shield between the personal assets of the business owner and a lawsuit judgment.

☐ *Miscellaneous Advantages.* You may find from an analysis of your own particular business that the corporate form will solve a problem unique to your business. For example, in some types of business, such as the construction business, it is expected that you will operate as a corporation. Banks, bonding companies, and other contractors may hesitate to deal with an unincorporated business. Additionally, some individuals feel that having a corporate name for their business will result in a greater amount of respect or prestige for their business.

Disadvantages of Incorporation

Cost

First, it is expensive when compared to a sole proprietorship or a partnership. At the time of this writing (1984), most attorneys are charging less than $75.00 to assist the owner of a sole proprietorship in forming his or her business. Primarily this involves the preparation of an assumed name certificate to be filed with the county clerk and advice on the different licenses required to operate the business. For a simple partnership the cost for a partnership agreement between the parties presently costs about $150.00.

However, for a corporation your costs can rise much higher. Today, most attorneys in small to medium-size cities are charging approximately the following amounts:

Filing fee to the state of Texas $300.00 + $10.00
handling fee

Printing fees for corporate
   book and documents   50.00
Attorney fees $250.00 to $500.00

Filing and printing fees are fairly standard. Table 1-1 is a partial listing of new filing fees for the state of Texas. However, the legal fees can and usually do vary from the low end of the range to the top end or higher because almost every business has some problems unique to it. The attorney has to evaluate how they are to be solved and how much time it will take. As a recommendation, if the attorney's fees exceed $500.00, do two things: question what needs to be done to warrant a higher fee and visit at least one other attorney regarding your incorporation. Chapter 2 offers additional information on how you should pick your attorney and what he should do for you.

Your Time and Effort

Incorporating your business takes a while. You will spend a considerable amount of time both in the formation and continued operation of the business. Almost like prescribing a diet, your attorney will set up a procedure you must follow to assure you the continued benefits of the corporate form. Such benefits can be lost if you do not follow his advice. This advice particularly relates to signing documents, making decisions and major purchases, and significant events in your business. Even though you know your business and its daily operation better than any attorney ever will, he knows how to document these activities to conform them to the corporate way of doing business. You must be flexible and take the extra time to do it right. There will also be some extra record keeping on your part.

Table 1-1
Partial Listing of Corporate Filing Fees

Articles of Incorporation	Fee
Business Corporation	$200 plus $100 franchise tax prepayment Total Fee:　$300
Professional Corporation	$200 plus $100 franchise tax prepayment Total Fee:　$300
Articles of Association for a Professional Association	$200
Name Reservation	$ 25
Articles of Amendment for a Professional Association	$100
Annual Statement for a Professional Association	$ 35
Articles of Dissolution for Business and Professional Corporations and Professional Associations	$ 25
Application for Reinstatement after forfeiture under the Texas Tax Code	$ 50
Assumed Name Certificate for an Incorporated Business or Profession	$ 25
Abandonment of Assumed Name for an Incorporated Business or Profession	$ 10

A Possible Tax Disadvantage

There are many different types of taxes that affect a corporation. Being a corporation in Texas will subject you to a franchise tax, which is just the tax on your being a corporation. It is usually minimal (under $100.00 per year). You may also notice a small increase in your social security taxes because you are no longer self-employed but are now an employee of the corporation. Also, if the business is operating at a loss, this could become a tax disadvantage; a loss cannot be carried over to your personal tax return. A company operating at a loss may resolve this problem by electing to be a Subchapter S corporation. (This election is discussed in Chapter 6.)

Table 1-2
Example of Incorporation Decision Maker

Advantages of Incorporation	Positive Points (1-10)	
Retirement plan	7	
Health, medical, disability insurance	9	
Medical reimbursement plan	5	
Term life insurance	3	
Corporate tax rates	8	
Business expenses	5	
Structured form of business	6	
Transfer of ownership	5	
Limited liability	10	
Other *having a corporate name*	4	
Total points		62

Disadvantages of Incorporation	Negative Points (1-10)	
Cost	8	
Additional time and effort	6	
Potential tax disadvantages	2	
Extra accounting	6	
Other _____	—	
Total points		22
Excess of *positive* over *negative* points		40

How to Decide To Incorporate

The decision to incorporate should be a joint effort between you, your attorney, and your accountant. Become involved in the decision; evaluate the advantages and disadvantages. After all, you are the one who must live with the new corporation from day to day. How do you best evaluate the factors in making this decision? One recommended method is to assign numerical values to each of the advantages and disadvantages previously discussed, or others that pertain to your particular situation. Since you know your business better than anyone else, you should assign a point value on a scale of one to ten to each factor depending on how important it is to you, one point for those of the least importance and ten for those of highest importance. (Table 1-2 is an example of this "incorporation decision-maker.") Then, compare the total "positive points" with the total "negative points." If you have more positive points over negative points, it *may* be in your best interest to consider an incorporation. Combine the results with the advice of your attorney and accountant, and then make your decision on incorporation. As a hint, read this entire book before you use such a chart. (There is much information in later chapters that may affect your decision.) Once you have done that, the chart will help assure that you have objectively evaluated both the pros and cons of the incorporation process.

Alternatives to Incorporation

After you evaluate the corporate form of business, you may decide that the corporation would not be beneficial for you or perhaps is not yet called for in your case. In this situation there are two other forms of business that may be appropriate for you, the *sole proprietorship* and the *partnership*.

If you alone are the owner of the new business, you may elect to become a sole proprietor. If you are already operating a one-person business, then this is your present form of business. As usually defined and previously mentioned in this chapter, this is one person operating a business for profit. It has some very good advantages and of course some disadvantages. The advantages that normally exist are:

1. It is very easy to form a sole proprietorship. Unlike the corporation, which requires fairly extensive legal work to form and operate, a sole proprietorship is basically formed by your personal decision to begin the business.
2. The sole proprietorship is subject to very little government regulation. A corporation is chartered by the state of Texas, and therefore the state has a continuing interest in your business. Therefore, you must report on an annual basis information on your business if you are incorporated. This is not the case in the sole proprietorship.
3. In that you are the only owner of the business, you have the greatest degree of flexibility in management and decision making. Your profits as well as your losses are totally yours.
4. Just as the sole proprietorship is very easy to form, it is also easy to dissolve. You of course remain personally liable on your debts and contracts, but you may dissolve your business simply by deciding to do so.

However, some of the disadvantages are large ones:

1. Perhaps the largest single disadvantage of a sole proprietorship lies in the area of legal liability. Since the business and you as an individual are one and the same, you are personally responsible for the debts and obligations of the business. If your business should fail and if there are not enough funds in the business to repay the debts of the business, your own personal property and funds (not protected by the Texas Homestead Act) may be taken by the creditors of the business to satisfy the debt. As explained previously, the corporate form of business is not subject to this disadvantage. The corporation's funds may be liable for the debts, but your per-

sonal funds are not. Your personal loss would be limited to the funds or property you invested in the corporation. This one disadvantage of sole proprietorship has convinced many new and existing businesses to adopt the corporate form.

2. From a management viewpoint, the sole proprietorship is a somewhat unstable form of business. Since its success depends on the work of only one person in its management, decision making, and operation, the business will probably not survive the death or incapacity of that one person. Simply stated, unless there is another person to step in and take over when the owner dies, the business dies with him. Banks and other financial institutions realize this, so it may be difficult to raise capital for the business. Employees realize this and are reluctant to establish a career with a sole proprietor. However, some of the same objections may very well extend to a one-person corporation.

Despite these disadvantages, the sole proprietorship does remain the most common form of business in the United States today. How long this will be the case is not known in that more and more sole proprietorships are being converted into the corporate form of business each year.

If you should desire to take the route of the sole proprietorship in Texas, the steps to legally establish yourself are very simple. You must first file an assumed name certificate with the county clerk of the county in which your business is located. Usually a call to your local county clerk will bring a form to you in the mail, or you may visit your county courthouse and complete the form there. It is then filed in the records of the county clerk and it is public notice that you are operating a business under a certain name.

The remaining step is to acquire whatever licenses that will be necessary to operate your business. Although the licenses required vary greatly depending upon the type of business you plan to establish, information on those required can often be obtained by contacting your city, county, or state government offices.

Your second option for a business form may be the *general partnership*. A partnership is two or more persons jointly engaging in a business for profit. It does have some distinct advantages such as the following:

1. It is easy to form a partnership and it does not require as much legal assistance as the formation of a corporation. There is, however, one very important document you should have and that is a written partnership agreement. (More on this later.)
2. Having a partner in your business may give you a wider range of management skills than you would have as a sole proprietorship. The different abilities of the partners will usually complement each other. One partner may be especially gifted in the area of sales while another partner may find the management area of the business more interesting.
3. Partnerships may find it easier to raise capital for the business. Since a lender would have more than one person to look toward for repayment of a loan, the partnership is a better credit risk for them.
4. Partnerships also have very little government regulation. Since they are established by the desires of the partners to engage in a business for profit and not by the state of Texas, the state has little interest in them.

However, there are again some disadvantages in this form of business:

1. Partnerships, like a sole proprietorship are characterized by the concept of unlimited liability. Just as in the

sole proprietorship, the partners are individually and personally liable for the debts of the business. If the partnership fails and does not have the funds to pay its debts, the creditors may and probably would look to the personal assets of the individual partners for payment. Since each partner has the right to incur debt in the name of the partnership, so long as it is in the normal course of operation, perhaps even without the knowledge of the remaining partners, you might become liable for a partnership debt totally without your knowledge. In essence, you must really know your partners before you join with them in a partnership. A corporation, as previously mentioned, does not have this disadvantage of unlimited liability, nor may one shareholder incur debt in the name of the corporation.

2. Another disadvantage, and probably the one that ends more partnerships than any other reason is the potential of disagreements between the partners. Partners can become very headstrong when it comes to making decisions, and if a disagreement cannot be resolved, it might mean the end of the partnership. Although partnerships are much easier than corporations to dissolve, there may be a conflict over the division of the property of the partnership.

If you should decide to follow the partnership route to doing business, its establishment is very similar to the sole proprietorship. You file an assumed name certificate with the county clerk of the county in which your partnership is located and obtain any licenses necessary to run your business. However, in addition to these steps, you should have a written partnership agreement. This partnership agreement sets forth in writing the agreements between the partners in relation to the operation, profit division, and dissolution of the partnership. Items usually considered in this agreement are:

1. The name of the partnership.
2. The purpose of the partnership.
3. How long the partnership will be in effect.
4. The location of the partnership's business.
5. How much investment will be made by each of the partners into the partnership.
6. How profits and losses of the partnership will be divided.
7. How and by whom will the partnership be managed.
8. Prohibited acts by partners. (Such as borrowing money or incurring debt in the partnership name without the agreement of the remaining partners.)
9. Under what circumstances and conditions may a new partner be admitted into the partnership.
10. Under what circumstances and conditions may an existing partner withdraw or retire from the partnership.
11. The disposal of a partner's interest in the partnership upon the death or disability of the partner.

In a well written partnership agreement, most of the difficult decisions that may someday face partners will have already been decided and agreed upon in this instrument. Partnerships without a written partnership agreement will have a much more difficult task in trying to resolve their operating problems after they have arisen. Figure 1-1 is a sample partnership agreement.

Before concluding our discussion of partnerships, there is an additional type of partnership that should be mentioned and that is the *limited partnership*. It is unlikely that a business would use this form of organization in that it is more appropriate to a group of investors holding or developing some type of investment property. However, in that you may have some dealings with a limited partnership, it should be explained. The limited partnership is a business form com-

(text continued on page 21)

Partnership Agreement

Benjamin Burns of *Harris* County, Texas, and *Robert Green* of *Harris* County, Texas, do hereby agree to form a general partnership on the terms and conditions set forth hereafter.

I. Name

The name of the partnership shall be *Burns & Green Home Care*.

II. Term of Partnership

The partnership shall begin on *November 1, 1984*, and shall continue until dissolved by the mutual agreement of the parties or until terminated pursuant to any agreement contained herein.

III. Purpose of Partnership

The partners shall work together for the purpose of conducting the business of *general residential contracting and construction*.

IV. Location of Business

The location of the business of the partnership shall be *1200 Hunt Street, Houston, Harris County*, Texas.

V. Partner Contributions

The total initial capital of the partnership shall be the amount of *$1,000.00*. Each partner shall contribute to the partnership the amount set forth below:

Benjamin Burns—$500.00
Robert Green   —$500.00

Figure 1-1. A partnership agreement such as this helps define operating procedures and avoid problems that can threaten a business's success.

Figure 1-1. (Continued on next page.)

VI. Profits & Losses

Each partner shall share profits or losses of the partnership in the following proportions:

Benjamin Burns—50%
Robert Green   —50%

VII. Time To Be Devoted by Partners

Each partner shall devote his undivided time and attention to the business and affairs of the partnership.

VIII. Management of the Partnership

Each partner shall have an equal voice in the management and affairs of the partnership. Each shall have the ability and authority to bind the partnership in the making of contracts and incurring obligations in the name of the partnership. However, no partner shall have the authority to bind the partnership for an obligation in excess of $1,000.00 without the written consent of the remaining partner. Any partner violating this provision shall be liable to the remaining partner for this obligation.

IX. Admission of New Partners

New partners may be admitted to the partnership only with the expressed consent of the existing partners.

X. Withdrawals by Partners

Each partner shall be allowed to withdraw from the partnership each month the hereinafter set amounts for their living expenses. At the conclusion of the partnership year, the total of the withdrawals for that year shall be charged against each partner's share of the profits for that year.

Benjamin Burns—$750.00
Robert Green   —$750.00

Figure 1-1. (Continued on next page.)

XI. Books and Records

The partnership shall keep accurate books and records of all transactions of the partnership. Said books shall be available for inspection by any partner during regular business hours. At the conclusion of the partnership year, financial statements shall be prepared and delivered to each partner and the net income or loss shall be allocated to each partner as agreed.

XII. Fiscal Year of the Partnership

The fiscal year for the partnership shall end on the *31st* day of *December* of each year.

XIII. Withdrawal or Retirement of a Partner

Any partner may withdraw or retire from the partnership at the conclusion of any fiscal year by giving the other partner *90* days' notice of his intent to do so.

XIV. Option to Purchase Interest of Withdrawing, Retiring, or Deceased Partner

In the event of the withdrawal, retirement, or death of a partner, the remaining partner may continue the business of the partnership and shall have the right and option to purchase the interest of the withdrawing, retiring, or deceased partner in the assets and goodwill of the business by paying to the partner or his legal representative the value of such interest as set forth hereinafter.

XV. Purchase Price of Partner's Interest

The purchase price of the withdrawing, retiring, or deceased partner's interest shall be determined by appraisal. The purchasing partner shall select one appraiser; and the selling partner, or the legal representative of a deceased partner, shall select a second appraiser. The purchase price to be paid shall be the amount jointly determined by the appraisers to be the value of the selling partner's inter-

Figure 1-1. (Continued on next page.)

est. In the event the two appraisers are unable to mutually agree on a purchase price, then the appraisers shall select a third appraiser whose appraisal shall be final and binding on the parties hereto.

XVI. Duties of Purchasing Partner

The purchasing partner shall assume all of the existing obligations and liabilities of the partnership and shall hold the withdrawing or retiring partner or the deceased partner's legal representative, heirs, and devisees free and harmless from all liability for said obligations. The name of the partnership may be continued to be used by the purchasing partner.

XVII. Dissolution of the Partnership

In the event the partnership shall be dissolved, the business affairs of the partnership shall be wound up, the partnership assets liquidated, the debts of the partnership paid, and any surplus then shall be divided between the partners in accordance with their interest in the partnership.

XVIII. Amendment of Partnership Agreement

This agreement is the sole and only agreement between the parties hereto. It may be amended by the mutual written consent of all partners hereto. Said amendment shall be attached to this original agreement.

Executed on *November 1, 1984*, at *Houston, Harris* County, Texas.

Signature of partner's
spouse:　　　　　　　　　　　Signature of Partners:

_____　　　　_____

Mary Burns　　　　　　　　　　Benjamin Burns, Partner

_____　　　　_____

Joan Green　　　　　　　　　　Robert Green, Partner

Figure 1-1. Continued.

bining some of the characteristics of both a partnership and a corporation. The individuals involved in a limited partnership are divided into two categories: general and limited partners. The general partners are the partners responsible for the management of the limited partnership. They have an unlimited liability for the debts and obligations of the partnership. The limited partners however are limited in their liability for debts and obligations of the partnership to the extent of their investment in the partnership. In turn, these limited partners have very little, if any, voice in how the partnership is managed. They are, in essence, silent partners. The limited partnership is most often used in Texas for real estate investment and developments. The limited partners are simply passive investors with no management authority. Limited partnerships are created somewhat like a corporation in that they must be filed with the state of Texas.

Summary

The decision to incorporate or not to incorporate should be made as you, a business person, would make any other business decision. That is, based on a careful evaluation of both the advantages and disadvantages as they apply to you. In most instances, the advantages of better retirement benefits, low corporate tax rates, insurance plans, limited liability, and a more defined and stable business form will outweigh the disadvantages of higher formation and maintenance costs, some remote tax disadvantages, and the greater amount of time required to properly operate a corporation.

These advantages and disadvantages should be explained to you by your attorney and your accountant, and these professionals should be of great assistance to you in your incorporation decision.

If you should decide that the corporate form of business is not appropriate for your business, there remain other forms of business you may use such as the sole proprietorship or the partnership. Both of these forms have positive and negative aspects. They are normally easier and less expensive to form than a corporation. From a negative standpoint, they suffer often from management problems and have the characteristic of unlimited personal liability for the debts and obligations of the business. By making a logical analysis of these business forms' advantages and disadvantages you can reach an intelligent decision on whether you should incorporate your business.

Chapter 2

You Can Do It Alone, But . . .

First, let us talk about the most often asked question, "Do I need an attorney to incorporate?" The answer is no, you do not. Every day people take care of their own legal matters. They write their own contracts, enter into agreements of their own making, and even take care of their own divorces. How well they do acting as their own attorney is the second question. The answer is, in general, poorly. Legal matters, like most other things in life, vary from the very simple to the most complex. You can easily take care of some matters, such as small claims court, yourself. Often, attorneys so advise their clients. However, other matters, including the incorporation of a business, fall into the more complex area. A mistake made by a person incorporating his own business could well cost much more than the fees of a good attorney.

It should not be stated absolutely that a person should not attempt his own incorporation. Given the time to research and work on the project, it can be done. If you are inclined to do so, this book will help you to resolve a majority of the problems you will face. However, if you are already running a business and your time is valuable, you may find it less expensive to employ a lawyer to incorporate you. Since he is in the business of incorporation, he is, from the standpoint of cost, the best person for the job. Secondly, with an attorney you have an assurance that the incorporation is done correctly.

Selecting the Right Attorney

Perhaps the most important decision, other than the one to incorporate, is the selection of the professionals who will assist you in the incorporation. For some this decision is not difficult. They have already used a certain attorney, and they have confidence in his judgment and ability. It is a foregone conclusion that this professional will assist them in their incorporation. If you already have a reliable attorney, all you need to do is to confirm that the tasks given to you later in this chapter have been accomplished.

However, many businesses have not used an attorney on a regular basis and must make a selection from the attorneys in their area. If you fall into this category, it is necessary to decide how you should evaluate and select your attorney.

First, consider the qualities your attorney should possess. The following are positive characteristics you should look for when you select your attorney. They are arranged in a checklist for you to follow. After the initial visit with your prospective attorney, but before you employ him or her, conduct an evaluation of these factors:

    Yes   No

1. ___ ___ Was your appointment and initial visit with the attorney handled in a profession and business-like manner?

2. ___ ___ Were you asked by the attorney to describe the present operation and future plans of your business?

3. ___ ___ Did the attorney summarize the characteristics
            of the corporate form of business, including
            those advantages and disadvantages discussed
            in Chapter 1?
4. ___ ___ Did the attorney describe the process of incor-
            poration on a step-by-step basis?
5. ___ ___ Did the attorney appear to be experienced and
            competent in the subject of incorporations?
6. ___ ___ Were the fees for the incorporation discussed
            with you and furnished to you in writing?
7. ___ ___ Were you given the opportunity to consider
            the attorney's proposals before making the de-
            cision to employ him?

Generally, all of the above should be answered *yes* after a
good incorporation interview. If you are not satisfied with
the interview, be a good legal consumer and visit with another attorney. Most attorneys know and understand that if
they assist a business in its incorporation, that business will
usually continue to use their services for its future legal
needs. Attorneys build their practice just as a business develops its customers. If the attorney does not seem to have the
time to spend on your incorporation needs, he probably will
not have time for your additional legal work.

Most experienced attorneys have developed the ability to
judge how much time a client's problem needs in order to be
correctly handled and explained to them, without using ex-
cessive time for which the client should not have to pay. This
is the one you are looking for, and the seven checklist items
will help you to find him.

Now that you know what criteria to look for in an attorney, how do you seek out that person? Here are some methods, listed in order of preference:

1. The best method to use is to ask for recommendations
   from other business people in your community that

have incorporated. Were they pleased with the work done for them and the time frame within which it was done? Was the attorney knowledgeable, accessible when needed, and interested in their incorporation? Were they fairly charged for the work done? If you receive a good recommendation based on these points, you have started in the right direction.

2. If you are unable to get a recommendation from another incorporated business and if you are located in or near a large city, you may contact one of the attorney referral services. These are no-charge services sponsored by local bar associations. Attorneys submit their name to the referral service along with the areas in which they normally practice. If you contact a service and indicate that you are seeking an attorney to assist you in an incorporation, you will be given the names of several local attorneys who work in this area. You may then arrange an interview, commonly at little or no charge, to evaluate the potential attorney according to the checklist. Do not assume that because you received several attorneys' names from the referral service that they are experts in incorporations. Approach and evaluate them just as you would any other attorney you might visit. The telephone numbers of attorney referral services are usually listed in the Yellow Pages of the telephone book under "Attorneys."

3. Assuming that you have neither a recommendation nor a referral service available, you may have to simply contact local attorneys by telephone and ask them if they perform incorporation work. You will usually find a very positive response from those law firms that work in this area and an invitation to visit with them and let them discuss your plans with you.

In many cases, the initial visit is done on a no-charge or very low charge basis. Since incorporations do differ from client to client, attorneys need the initial interview as much as you do to help them decide if they can assist you. Since many attorneys consider the first meeting to be mutual evaluation, they charge no fee for it. This, however, is a point you need to ask about in your first telephone contact.

What Your Attorney Should Do for You

Once you have found the right attorney, what are the things you should expect to have done in the incorporation? The following are steps that should be done by your attorney to correctly perform an incorporation. This is not an all inclusive listing. There may be items that are unique to your business and called for in addition to the listed items. The purpose of the listing is to show steps that should be done and items that should be furnished to you that you will easily recognize. If an item is missing or a step overlooked, ask about it. These necessary elements should not be omitted:

1. Your proposed name should be checked for availability for use with the secretary of state of Texas. As discussed later, this means you are free to use such a name for your corporation.
2. Articles of incorporation should be prepared. This document, a copy of which is included in Chapter 3, is submitted in two duplicate copies to the secretary of state of Texas in Austin along with your filing fee. One copy is returned to you by the state along with the certificate of incorporation.
3. A corporation book should be prepared for you. This is usually a binder containing your corporation minutes, bylaws, stock certificates, and other legal papers.
4. The attorney should hold your first organization meeting with you. Some attorneys merely have their clients

sign a consent to act without a meeting, and this procedure may be appropriate where the incorporators find
it difficult to meet. However, the best practice is to
have an actual meeting.
5. There are usually some final details. In most incorporations there are additional items such as leases, assumed name certificates, buy-sell agreements, etc. that
need to be prepared. These should be furnished before
the incorporation is completed.

Your Need for an Accountant

If you have been operating an established business, one
basic need has probably been met: the services of an accountant or bookkeeper. Where this is the case, the transition
to incorporation will be fairly easy for you from an accounting standpoint. Remember to keep your accountant fully informed about your incorporation plans in order to help you
plan the timing of the changeover and the tax decisions to be
made. Because of the steadily increasing number of corporations in Texas, most accountants are experienced with their
accounting and tax problems. Therefore, assuming you are
satisfied with the work being done presently by your accountant, you will not need to change accountants.

For the business enterprise that has not used an accountant, here is a suggestion. While the incorporation is being
performed, seek out and hire a person to help you with accounting and tax preparation. Select an accountant in the
same manner recommended for selecting an attorney. A recommendation from another business person is the best
method. If you cannot get any recommendations, visit some
accountants in your area.

Once you have selected a potential accountant, meet with
him and describe what your business will involve. Evaluate

your accountant as you would your attorney, but keep one additional point in mind. Once the incorporation is concluded, most of the attorney's work is done, but from then on the accountant really begins to work for you. Since accounting is a process of record keeping and data collection on a daily basis, a relationship with an accountant will be on a regular basis. Select an accountant as you would a wife; pick someone you can get along with.

As your business begins to function and grow, you will need to decide how much work you want your accountant to do and how much you can perform yourself. Good accountants are not cheap. Although you will need their services to establish a set of "books" for your business, ideally you or someone within the firm should have the ability to record daily transactions in some organized manner (such as on a daily report form) so that the accountant's services are needed only at the end of each month and year to summarize data and prepare financial statements. This is the most economical method for using the services of an accountant. The development of this shared responsibility between you and your accountant will take some time and effort. Be patient, and it will gradually define itself.

One final word on accountants. Not all accountants are certified public accountants. Although some are not C.P.A.'s and may call themselves a bookkeeping service, tax service, or business service, do not exclude them from consideration. There are many individuals who are very competent in accounting and tax services who are not certified public accountants. Generally, their fees are lower, and they direct their work toward smaller and beginning businesses. Your accounting needs may be thoroughly serviced by a non-certified accountant. However, you must remember that certified public accountants have passed a very rigorous examination in accounting and tax practice and have satisfied an experience requirement before being certified. These conditions give you a very high degree of assurance that they are qualified and competent. For a business with complex and difficult tax and accounting problems, a certified public accountant may be your best choice.

Summary

The selection of the right attorney and accountant to assist you in your incorporation is most important. Although a non-attorney may successfully incorporate a business, from the standpoint of time and cost it will most often be to your benefit to seek professional assistance. In seeking the right attorney, a number of positive characteristics should be apparent to you from your initial visit with the attorney. In that this may be the most important legal experience your business will encounter, look for the characteristics of experience, interest, explanation, and fairness of fees. Do not hesitate to consult another attorney if you are not completely satisfied with your interview experience.

Use the recommendations of other business people in the community to seek out your attorney and accountant. Also consider the referral services available in larger cities or simply visit with attorneys and accountants local to your area.

From the information you will gain from this book, establish the tasks you expect your attorney to complete for you and question the omission of any of these tasks. Those professionals selected by you will appreciate your interest in the incorporation process. In that most attorneys and accountants develop their practice on a referral basis from other satisfied clients, they will make every effort to successfully meet your legal and accounting needs.

Chapter 3

The Procedure of Incorporation

To this point, consideration has been given to some preliminary items relative to a corporation, its advantages and disadvantages, and how you might select the right attorney and accountant to assist in the process of incorporation. Now it is necessary to look at the actual incorporation procedure, which may be divided into three phases:

Phase One —gathering initial information and preparation of the articles of incorporation.
Phase Two —conducting the organizational meeting of the corporation's board of directors.
Phase Three—preparation of the corporate book.

Phase Two and Three are sometimes done in reverse order. Which one happens first is not as material as the fact that both should take place. Since what is going to happen in the organizational meeting of a small corporation is often completely predictable, all of the documents—minutes, bylaws, stock certificates, etc.—can be prepared in advance. By doing this, when the meeting is completed, so is the incorporation.

Phase One—Articles of Incorporation

The articles of incorporation is the document that is filed with the secretary of state of Texas in application for a certificate of incorporation for a new company. The certificate of incorporation is the instrument that creates the corporation and gives it legal life.

Perhaps the best way to illustrate this process is to use a hypothetical example. Benjamin Burns and his partner, Robert Green, are beginning a new business in the home repair field. After consideration of the corporate form, they elect to incorporate. They select an attorney, who prepares for them the articles of incorporation shown in Figure 3-1.

This is the form recommended by the office of the secretary of State of Texas. The underlined portions of the form are those that are changed from client to client. Two copies of the document are signed and notarized and forwarded to the secretary of state in Austin along with the filing fee of $310.00. Usually within two to three days you will receive a telephone call from the secretary of state's office to let you know that the articles of incorporation are filed and the certificate of incorporation is being issued. At the point of the issue of the certificate of incorporation, the corporation begins to exist.

The meaning and purpose of the articles should be clearly understood. References hereinafter are to statutes in the Business Corporation Act as contained in Vernon's Texas Civil Statutes. This is the set of lawbooks that contains the laws of the state of Texas. Most college and larger public libraries have a set of these books. Volume 3A contains the Business Corporation Act and the laws that regulate the forming of a corporation.

Article One establishes the legal name of the corporation. As simple as it may appear, this step often takes a great deal of thought on the part of incorporators. In an already established business, the owners will usually desire to use the present name of the firm for its incorporated name. This may or may not be possible for reasons examined later. If the business is just beginning, then deciding on a name may be more difficult. Different people have different opinions of what makes a good business name. I suggest you keep it short and modest and see that the initials do not spell something undesirable. Select first, second, and third choice names for your new corporation.

You will not always be able to incorporate under your favorite name. No two corporations in Texas may have exactly the same name. Nor may two have names that are similar without the consent of the corporation that used the name first. Article 2.05 of the Business Corporation Act states the following:

Art. 2.05. Corporate Name; Use of Assumed Names

  A. The Corporate name shall conform to the following requirements:

    (1) It shall contain the word "corporation," "company," or "incorporated," or shall contain an abbreviation of one of such words, and shall contain such additional words as may be required by law.

    (2) It shall not contain any word or phrase which indicates or implies that it is organized for any purpose other than one or more of the purposes contained in its articles of incorporation. .

    (3) It shall not be the same as, or deceptively similar to, the name of any domestic corporation existing under the laws of this State, or the name of any foreign corporation authorized to transact business in this State, or a name the exclusive right to which is, at the time, reserved in the manner provided in this Act, or the name of a corporation which has in effect a registration of its corporate name as provided in this Act; provided that a

Articles of Incorporation

Article One

The name of the corporation is <u>Burns and Green Home Care, Inc.</u>

Article Two

The period of its duration is *perpetual.*

Article Three

The purpose for which the corporation is organized is the transaction of any or all lawful business for which corporations may be incorporated under the Texas Business Corporation Act.

Article Four

The aggregate number of shares which the corporation shall have authority to issue is <u>one million (1,000,000) of the par value of one dollar ($1.00) each.</u>

Article Five

The corporation will not commence business until it has received for the issuance of shares consideration of the value of one thousand dollars ($1,000.00) consisting of money, labor done, or property actually received.

Article Six

The street address of its initial registered office is <u>1200 Hunt Street, Houston, Texas 77001,</u> and the name of its registered agent at such address is <u>Benjamin Burns.</u>

Figure 3-1. (Continued on next page.)

Article Seven

The number of directors constituting the initial board of directors is *two*, and the names and addresses of the person or persons who are to serve as directors until the first annual meeting of the shareholders or until their successors are elected and qualified are:

Benjamin Burns—Houston, Texas
Robert Green —Houston, Texas

Article Eight

The name and address of the incorporator is:

Benjamin Burns—Houston, Texas

_____
Benjamin Burns, Incorporator

THE STATE OF TEXAS
COUNTY OF HARRIS

Before me, a notary public, on this day personally appeared Benjamin Burns, known to me to be the person whose name is subscribed to the foregoing document and, being by me first duly sworn, declared that the statements therein contained are true and correct.

Given under my hand and seal of office this ____ day of _____, 198__.

_____
Notary Public, State of Texas

(Seal)   My commission expires:
_____, 19__.

Figure 3-1. This is a typical example of the articles of incorporation your attorney would file with the secretary of state of Texas.

name may be similar if written consent is obtained from the existing corporation having the
name deemed to be similar or the person, or corporation, for whom the name deemed to be similar is reserved in the office of the Secretary of
State.

B. Any domestic or foreign corporation having authority
to transact business in this State, may do so under an
assumed name, by filing an assumed name certificate
in the manner prescribed by law.

As stated in part (1), the corporation name shall contain
words noting that it is a corporation. It may be upsetting to a
business person who has operated under a name for years to
learn that the name is not available for the new corporation.
The fact is whoever incorporated under a name first probably has the right to use it. If names are somewhat similar but
not exactly alike, then, as part (3) states, with a letter of consent from the first corporation the new corporation may
adopt a similar name.

There is, however, another method allowed by paragraph
B of the article that will allow a new corporation to use its
old name, even though that name might not be available for
incorporation. You simply incorporate the business under a
legally available name and then file an assumed name certificate with the county clerk and office of the secretary of
state. Assuming the corporation that has your desired name
is unaffected by a new company's use of the name, the two
companies may co-exist without any problem. To determine
whether a corporation name is available, you may call the
secretary of state's office in Austin (area code (512) 475-
3551). The answering operator has a computer terminal
available and will usually respond quickly that the name is
available, not available, or available with a letter of consent.
The operator can be very helpful and will usually check as
many as three names for you per telephone call. Such calls
are answered on working days between 8:00 a.m. and 5:00
p.m.

TO THE SECRETARY OF STATE
OF THE STATE OF TEXAS:

Pursuant to the provisions of Article 2.06 of the Texas Business Corporation Act, the undersigned hereby applies for reservation of the following corporate name for a period of one hundred twenty days:

BURNS & GREEN HOME CARE, INC.

Dated _____, 1984.

_____
Benjamin Burns

THE STATE OF TEXAS
COUNTY OF *HARRIS*

Before me, a notary public, on this day personally appeared *Benjamin Burns,* known to me to be the person whose name is subscribed to the foregoing document and, being by me first duly sworn, declared that the statements therein contained are true and correct.

Given under my hand and seal of office this ____ day of _____, A.D., *1984.*

_____
(Printed or stamped name)
Notary Public, State of Texas
My commission expires:

(Seal)

_____, 19____.

Figure 3-2. This form, when filed with the secretary of state of Texas, reserves your corporate name and prohibits it from being used by another incorporating business for 120 days.

If your preferred name is available but your articles of incorporation are not to be immediately filed, you may reserve that chosen name by filing with the secretary of state of Texas a reservation of corporate name. This filing reserves for 120 days the name you have selected and prohibits it from being selected and used by another incorporating business. A form for the reservation of corporate name as promulgated by the office of the secretary of state of Texas is shown in Figure 3-2.

Article Two states how long the corporation will exist. Unless there is reason to limit the corporation's life, you want to use a perpetual duration. This provision means that the corporation will continue to exist until some action is taken to dissolve it.

Article Three requires a brief historical example. In the past it was the practice to use a fairly limited and narrow purpose clause for the corporation. For instance, a few years ago a small crop dusting corporation in South Texas might have had the following purpose clause, "To engage in the business of the sale and aerial application of chemicals to crops and to purchase, maintain, and sell aircraft capable of such application." This description worked well until the owners wanted to engage in a farming operation. Since the purpose of the corporation was so restrictive about what the corporation could engage in, the new operation was not possible. Today, by using a general purpose clause, owners of a corporation may expand their business activities into unrelated fields and still be within their purpose clause.

Article Four helps to establish the potential capital structure of the corporation. Notice the phrase "potential capital." The Burns and Green corporation has the legal ability to issue up to 1,000,000 shares of stock at a minimum price of $1.00 per share. It may well be that this amount of stock will never be issued, but the ability is there.

Article Five established the minimum investment to be made in a corporation before it may become active. Our Texas law states the following:

Art. 3.05. Requirement Before Commencing Business

A. A corporation shall not transact any business or incur any indebtedness, except such as shall be incidental to its organization or to obtaining subscriptions to or payment for its shares, until it has received for the issuance of shares consideration of the value of at least One Thousand Dollars ($1,000.00), consisting of money, labor done, or property actually received.

Simply stated, this minimum capital must be invested before the corporation may begin business. Notice that the statute states "money, labor done, or property actually received." Therefore, you may meet the requirements of the statute by doing one of the following:

1. Deposit a minimum of $1,000.00 in the corporation name in a bank account.
2. Once the certificate of incorporation has been issued, perform labor for the corporation having a fair value of $1,000.00
3. Transfer property to the corporation with a minimum value of $1,000.00.

Most incorporators deposit cash to start a new business. In an existing business situation, the owners should inventory all the items that are being transferred to the new corporation and transfer them into the corporation by a bill of sale. In return for the cash or items transferred into the business, the new owners will receive stock in the corporation. Remember that the amount transferred into the corporation may be any amount as long as it is more than $1,000.00. Later in the chapter, the transfer and method of determining the amount of stock to be received will be described.

Article Six sets forth the registered agent and office of the corporation. Texas law states:

Art. 2.09. Registered Office and Registered Agent
  A. Each corporation shall have and continually maintain in this State:
     (1) A registered office which may be, but need not be, the same as its place of business.
     (2) A registered agent, which agent may be either an individual resident in this State whose business office is identical with such registered office, or a domestic corporation, or a foreign corporation authorized to transact business in this State which has a business office identical with such registered office.

This registered agent is simply the person the state may contact to communicate with the corporation. If after the corporation has been formed there is a change in the address of the registered agent, or another person is to be registered agent, it is important to file a change of registered agent, address or both with the office of the secretary of the state of Texas.

Article Seven covers the preliminary board of directors for the corporation. What is their purpose? State law says:

Art. 2.31. Board of Directors
  A. The business and affairs of a corporation shall be managed by a board of directors. Directors need not be residents of this State or shareholders of the corporation unless the articles of incorporation or bylaws so require. The articles of incorporation or bylaws may prescribe other qualifications for directors.

The directors set forth in the articles will serve as such until a new board of directors is elected.

Last of all, Article Eight names the incorporators. Article 3.01 of the Business Corporation Act says:

Art. 3.01. Incorporators
A. Any natural person of the age of eighteen (18) years or more, or any partnership, corporation, association, trust, or estate (without regard to place of residence, domicile, or organization) may act as an incorporator of a corporation by signing and verifying the articles of incorporation for such corporation and by delivering the original and a copy of the articles of incorporation to the Secretary of State.

Even though there may be several parties involved in the corporation, only one incorporator is needed. Once the articles of incorporation are completed, signed, and filed, your corporation is now in existence. Article 3.03 states:

Art. 3.03. Filing of Articles of Incorporation
A. The original and a copy of the articles of incorporation shall be delivered to the Secretary of State. If the Secretary of State finds that the articles of incorporation conform to law, he shall, when all fees have been paid as required by law:
(1) Endorse on the original and the copy the word "Filed," and the month, day, and year of the filing thereof.
(2) File the original in his office.
(3) Issue a certificate of incorporation to which he shall affix the copy.
B. The certificate of incorporation, together with the copy of the articles of incorporation affixed thereto by the Secretary of State, shall be delivered to the incorporators or their representatives.

John A. Barrister
Attorney at Law

Secretary of State
Corporate Division
Special Handling
P.O. Box 12436
Austin, Texas 78711
RE: ARTICLES OF INCORPORATION FOR *BURNS &*
       GREEN HOME CARE, INC.
Dear Sir:
   Enclosed please find the original and a copy of Articles of
Incorporation for *Burns & Green Home Care, Inc.*
   Also enclosed is our firm check in the amount of $300.00
made payable to the Secretary of State for both the initial
franchise tax deposit and the statutory filing fee. Further,
please find enclosed our firm check for $10.00 for the spe-
cial handling fee.
                                    Yours very truly,

                                    John A. Barrister, Attorney
JAB/mdh
Enclosures

*Figure 3-3. This is an example of a letter that would accom-
pany the articles of incorporation to the secretary of state of
Texas.*

   The certificate of incorporation and one copy of the articles of incorporation will be returned for your corporate records. An example of a letter that should accompany the articles of incorporation to the office of the secretary of state is
shown in Figure 3-3. Figure 3-4 is the checklist formerly
used by the secretary of state to check submitted articles of
incorporation for required information. Although checklists
are no longer used, they remain a valuable guide for us.

Date   Name
Need $_____   Refund $_____
☐ Is the name available?
☐ Is the name identical in Heading and Article I?
☐ Is COMPANY, CORPORATION, INCORPO-
RATED, or CO., CORP., INC., included in the
name?
☐ Is the term of existence set out?
☐ Is the par value of shares stated, or else that
shares have no par value?
☐ Is there a statement that the corporation will not
commence business until it has received at
least $1,000.00 for the issuance of shares?
☐ Is the building or street address or rural route
address of its registered office in Texas given?
☐ Is the registered agent named? (Must be at the
same address as registered office)
☐ Is there at least one director? Is his address
shown?
☐ Is there at least one incorporator? Is his address shown? (At least City and State) (Any natural person of the age of 18, or any partnership,
corporation, association, trust or estate without
regard to residence may act as an incorporator)
☐ Did all the incorporators sign?
☐ Did all the incorporators verify? (Sworn or under oath)
☐ Is notary seal, signature, and date on verification?
☐ Do we have duplicate originals of the articles?
☐ Is duplicate signed and verified with genuine
notary seal and signatures and verification
date, all identical to original?

Figure 3-4. This checklist, formerly used by the office of the secretary of state to approve the articles of incorporation is a helpful guide for collecting information.

Article 3.04 describes the effect of the issuance of the certificate of incorporation:

Art. 3.04. Effect of Issuance of Certificate of Incorporation
A. Upon the issuance of the certificate of incorporation, the corporate existence shall begin, and such certificate of incorporation shall be conclusive evidence that all conditions precedent required to be performed by the incorporators have been compiled with and that the corporation has been incorporated under this Act, except as against the State in a proceeding for involuntary dissolution.

Phase One is now completed. Normally the completion of the incorporation process to this point presents no problems and is correctly performed whether done by an attorney or someone performing his own incorporation. However, there is a tendency, especially among those who have prepared their own articles, to stop at this point and not complete the process. The remaining steps of the process are critical; they are the steps in which the judgment and expertise of an attorney will be most valuable to you.

Phase Two—The Organizational Meeting

What is the organizational meeting and how is it conducted? Article 3.06 states

Art 3.06. Organization Meeting of Directors
A. After the issuance of the certificate of incorporation, an organization meeting of the initial board of directors named in the articles of incorporation shall be held, either within or without this State, at the call of a majority of the directors named in the articles of incorporation, for the purpose of adopting bylaws, electing officers, and transacting such other business as may come before the meeting. The directors call-

ing the meeting shall give at least three (3) days notice thereof by mail to each director so named, stating
the time and place of the meeting.

The ideal time to have the organizational meeting is as
soon as possible after the certificate of incorporation is issued.

Phase Three—The Corporate Book

Preparing the corporate book involves several steps. Remember that the term "book" does not refer to accounting
books, such as the general journal and general ledger. The
corporate book is the official record of the formation and operation of the corporation from a legal standpoint. It should
be prepared by the attorney performing the incorporation
and presented to you at the time the corporation is completed. Keep it in a safe and secure place, perhaps next to the
family Bible.

Most attorneys purchase corporate books for their clients
from several printers. There are now so many Texas corporations that these printers have prepared special editions of
their corporate books that are customized for use in Texas.
Most office supply companies can order these corporate
books for you.

The corporate book contains, in addition to specially written documents called for in a particular client's business, the
following documents:

1. Written minutes of the organizational meeting of the directors of the corporation.
2. The original certificate of incorporation.
3. The corporation bylaws.
4. A book of printed stock certificates.
5. A stockholder's ledger listing all shareholders.

Each year the minutes of the annual meeting and the consents (which will be discussed later) are placed in the corporate book and act as a recorded history of the activities of the corporation.

A Typical Organizational Meeting

Here is how a typical organizational meeting might be conducted for a small corporation. The minutes of the meeting are a written description of these actions and would be prepared after the meeting or perhaps even before the meeting if the preparer knows exactly what is to take place at the meeting. The notice previously referred to may have been sent by mail to the directors. More often, however, the directors sign a waiver of having to receive the notice, and it is not given. Actually, the simple attendance of a director at the meeting waives the required notice unless he or she is present to object to the meeting taking place.

Consider again the previously mentioned home repair company, Burns & Green Home Care, Inc. A certificate of incorporation has been issued and the corporation is in existence—now for their organizational meeting. The meeting will usually take place at either the place of business or the attorney's office. After the minutes of the organizational meeting are written, they might appear as follows. (There are various *Note*'s and explanations in this example that would not appear in the actual minutes.)

Minutes of the Organization Meeting
of
Burns & Green Home Care, Inc.

On the ____ day of _____, 19__, the organizational meeting of the directors of Burns & Green Home Care, Inc. was held at 1200 Hunt Drive, Houston, Texas. Present at the meeting were Benjamin Burns and

Robert Green who are the initial directors of the corporation. Also present was John Barrister, attorney for the corporation. Presented to the meeting was the signed waiver of notice of the meeting signed by all directors of the corporation. It was then declared that the meeting was legally and correctly called and open for business. It was directed that the signed waiver should be placed with these minutes in the corporate book of the corporation.

1. Chairman and secretary of the meeting. It was agreed and resolved that Benjamin Burns would act as the chairman of the meeting and Robert Green would serve as secretary.
2. Report of the incorporation. It was reported to the meeting that the articles of incorporation of the new corporation were filed by the secretary of state of Texas and that a certificate of incorporation was issued on _____, 19__. It was resolved that the articles and certificate of incorporation be placed in the corporate book of the corporation.
3. Election of officers of the corporation. The following persons were nominated and elected as officers of the corporation:

Benjamin Burns—President
Robert Green   —Secretary

Note: Regarding officers, Article 2.42 of the act states:

Art. 2.42. Officers
A. The officers of a corporation shall consist of a president, one or more vice-presidents as may be prescribed by the bylaws, a secretary, and a treasurer, each of whom shall be elected by the board of directors at such time and in such manner as may be prescribed by the bylaws. Such other officers and assistant officers and agents as may be deemed necessary may be elected or appointed by the board of directors or chosen in such other manner as may be prescribed by the bylaws.

Any two (2) or more offices may be held by the same person.

B. All officers and agents of the corporation, as between themselves and the corporation, shall have such authority and perform such duties in the management of the corporation as may be provided in the bylaws, or as may be determined by resolution of the board of directors not inconsistent with the bylaws.

4. Resolutions of the board of directors. The following matters were brought up for discussion, considered, and the following resolutions were passed by the board of directors:

   a. Bylaws. It is resolved that the corporation adopt the bylaws as presented to the meeting and said bylaws are to be placed in the corporate minute book.

   b. Stock certificate. It is resolved that the form of stock certificate as presented to the meeting be adopted as the official certificate of the corporation.

   c. Corporate seal. It is resolved that the corporate seal as presented to the meeting be adopted as the official seal of the corporation. An impression of the seal is to be made upon the minutes herein.
   Note: Corporate seals are no longer required by law. However, their use has continued in Texas and most corporations adopt a seal. The seal is a small hand stamp or impression, much like a notary seal that contains the name of the corporation and the date of incorporation.

   d. Corporation bank account. It is resolved that the corporation establish a bank account with the Ship Channel Bank of Houston, Texas.
   Note: Most banks have their own form of bank resolution to establish a bank account for your corporation. The language of the bank's resolution may be copied here in the minutes.

e. Minute book. It is resolved that the corporate minute book as presented to the meeting is adopted as
the official minute book of the corporation.

f. Issue of stock. It is resolved that the consideration
transferred into the corporation for shares of stock
in the corporation is fair and adequate consideration as determined by the board of directors and
the shares as set forth hereinafter should be issued
to the shareholders as shown:

Name of Shareholder	Number of Shares	Consideration Paid
Benjamin Burns	500	$500.00
Robert Green	500	$500.00

Note: The issue of stock is a very important part of your corporate minutes. As stated in Article 3.05 of the Business Corporation Act, a minimum of $1,000.00 must be received by the cor-
poration prior to its starting business. If cash is the consideration
to be transferred to the corporation in return for stock, this is
simple to document as shown in the example. Since each share of
stock has a par value of $1.00, then for $500.00 we would receive 500 shares of stock. For rather complex reasons when you
have a stock with a par value, the value assigned to each share
when you begin a corporation must be at par or above, never be-
low. The corporation bank account will show the $1,000.00 hav-
ing been received by the corporation.

However, Article 3.05 also permits the initial $1,000.00 to be
in the form of labor done or property received, or perhaps a combination of all of these. This makes the initial capitalization
somewhat more complicated because a value is not so easily
placed on labor or property as it is on a monetary item such as
cash. If property is being received by the corporation, a detailed
inventory of the property along with a fair market value should
be placed in the minutes. If labor is done, then the labor should
be valued at a fair value and should have been done after the cer-

tificate of incorporation was filed. If we changed our example
and had Mr. Burns contributing tools and Mr. Green contributing
labor, the situation would be described as follows:

Name of Shareholder	Number of Shares	Consideration
Benjamin Burns	500	Property having a fair market value of $500.00; see attachment A.
Robert Green	500	Labor done for corporation having a fair value of $500.00; see attachment B.

Attachment A

Property contributed	Fair Market Value
One (1) Table Saw Serial #001	$250.00
One (1) Electric Drill Serial #002	50.00
One (1) Lot cabinet hardware	200.00
Total	$500.00

Attachment B

Labor Contributed
50 hours spent in promotion of corporation by visiting builders, job sites
and retail stores at $10.00 per hour. $500.00

5. Adjournment of the meeting. No other business having
   been brought before this organizational meeting of the
   board of directors, this meeting was declared to be adjourned.

Dated and approved _____, 19____.

_____
Chairman

_____
Secretary

Waiver of Notice
Organizational Meeting of Board of Directors
of
Burns & Green Home Care, Inc.

We, the undersigned, being the initial directors of the above corporation do hereby waive having to receive notice of the organizational meeting of the corporation and do hereby consent that said meeting may be held at _____ , Texas on _____ , 19____ , at the hour of _____ .M. and all necessary business may be transacted at that time.

Dated _____ , 19____ .

_____
Benjamin Burns

_____
Robert Green

Additional Actions To Be Considered at the Corporate Meeting

Depending upon the size, number of people involved, and the complexity of the corporation, there may be additional matters the beginning corporation should consider. The nature of these matters makes them more complex, and they need to be evaluated by your attorney to determine if they are necessary and if they should be included in your organizational meeting. They include such matters as:

□ *Adoption of Shareholders' Buy-Sell Agreement* (sometimes called stock purchase agreement). The essence of such an agreement is that if a stockholder decides to sell his investment, he must first offer it to the remaining shareholders and give them the option to purchase his stock. The agreement also provides that in the event of the death of a shareholder, the other shareholders of the corporation shall have the right to purchase the stock of the deceased shareholder at a preset price. This arrangement eliminates one of the greatest problems in a small corporation: the death of a shareholder whose stock is inherited by a spouse who has no connection with the business nor any idea what the stock is worth. It can sometimes take years to settle one of these problems.

☐ *Adoption of Employment Agreements.* If a corporation is going to pay a salary to a person who is perhaps also a shareholder, officer, and director, this procedure is best carried out by a written employment agreement approved by the board of directors in their meeting and recorded in the minutes.

☐ *Legal Notices.* If the incorporated business was previously doing business as a sole proprietorship or partnership and if the same former name is to be used by the corporation, a legal notice must be published in a local newspaper (one published in the same county as the corporation) once a week for four weeks. This is public notice that the former business is now a corporation and has the benefits of such, especially that of limited liability. In addition, if a company being incorporated normally has an inventory, notices may be necessary to comply with the Texas Bulk Sales Act.

☐ *Incorporation Under the Section 1244 Plan.* Section 1244 of the Internal Revenue Code provides that a loss suffered on stock purchased under such plan may be treated as an ordinary loss instead of a capital loss on your tax return, thus producing a tax benefit.

The Corporation Bylaws

In the model corporation, provision was made for the adoption of bylaws in the organizational meeting of the corporation. Bylaws are simply the operating rules and guidelines of the corporation. They may provide for the election of directors and officers, explain how meetings are called and conducted, regulate voting of shares, etc. In most instances the corporation book prepared by the attorney will include printed bylaws that are adopted and customized for each particular corporation. Bylaws are usually very lengthy, and an example set for our model corporation is shown in Appendix B at the end of this book.

Shareholders, Directors, and Officers

In discussions to this point all three of these terms have been used, so it would be well to specifically define them and their duties. Remember that corporations may range from a one-person corporation, in which that one person holds all three positions, to very large corporations, where different people occupy these positions.

☐ *Shareholder* (also stockholder). This is the owner, or one of many owners, of a corporation. Ownership of a Texas corporation is reflected by stock that has been issued to a stockholder.

☐ *Director.* This is the person(s) who actually manages the business and affairs of the corporation. Stated in a different way, the director(s) creates policy for the corporation, defines what the corporation should do, and directs how it should be done.

☐ *Officers.* These are the persons charged with the responsibility of the daily operation of the corporation. They carry out the policy and management as dictated by the director(s).

A Texas corporation must have two officers, the president and secretary, although in reality they may be the same person.

All of this may seem somewhat ridiculous in the incorporation of a one- or two-person business. Since one person can be both shareholder, director and officer, why have so many positions to complicate an apparently simple matter? The answer lies in the history of Texas corporations. In the not-so-distant past, most companies did not incorporate until they had grown quite large in operation. There were usually a large number of shareholders, most of whom were not involved in the business. In this situation there was a need for a board of directors to represent the shareholders and create "policy" and a small group, the officers, to carry it out. However, in the last few years, with more and more small businesses incorporating to seek the corporate advantages, a situation has arisen wherein a smaller business operates with formalities more appropriate to a larger one.

Texas has made a good faith effort to modernize this situation by the passage of its close corporation statute, Article 12.32 which provides, in part:

 A. Close Corporation Provisions. All shareholders of a close corporation may make one or more shareholders' agreements. The business and affairs of a close corporation or the relations among the shareholders that may be regulated by a shareholders' agreement include without limitation:

  (1) management of the business and affairs of the close corporation with or without a board of directors, by its shareholders, or in whole or part by one or more of its shareholders or by one or more persons not shareholders;

  (2) buy-sell, first option, first refusal, or similar arrangements with respect to the close corporation's shares or other securities, and restrictions on their transfer, including restrictions beyond

those permitted to be imposed by Article 2.22 of this Act;

(3) declaration and payment of dividends and other distributions, whether or not in proportion to ownership of shares, in amounts permitted by this Act or the manner in which profits or losses shall be apportioned;

(4) restrictions on the rights of a transferee of shares or assignee to participate in the management or administration of the close corporation's business and affairs during the term of the shareholders' agreement;

(5) rights of one or more shareholders to dissolve the close corporation at will or on the occurrence of a specified event or contingency in which case the dissolution of the close corporation shall proceed as if all of its shareholders had consented in writing to dissolution of the close corporation as provided by Article 6.02 of this Act;

(6) exercise or division of voting power either in general or in regard to specified matters by or among the shareholders of the close corporation or other persons, including without limitation:

    (a) voting agreements and voting trusts that need not conform with Article 2.30 of this Act;

    (b) requiring the vote or consent of the holders of a greater or lesser number of shares than is otherwise required by this Act or other law, including any action for termination of close corporation status;

    (c) granting one or some other specified number of votes for each shareholder; and

    (d) permitting any action for which this Act requires approval by the vote of the board of directors or by a vote of the shareholders of an ordinary corporation or by both, to be taken without such a vote, in the manner provided in the shareholders' agreement;

(7) terms and conditions of employment of any shareholder, director, officer, or other employee of the close corporation, regardless of the length of the period of employment;

(8) the natural persons who shall be directors, if any, and officers of the close corporation;

(9) arbitration of issues about which the shareholders may become deadlocked in voting or about which the directors or those empowered to manage the close corporation may become deadlocked and the shareholders are unable to break the deadlock;

(10) termination of close corporation status, including any right of dissent or other rights that shareholders who object to the termination may be granted;

(11) qualifications of persons who are or are not entitled to be shareholders of the close corporation;

(12) amendments to or termination of the shareholders' agreement; and

(13) any provision required or permitted by this Act to be set forth in the bylaws.

The close corporation concept is a good one. Its aim is to simplify corporate management and provide for less formality in small corporations. However, as is the case with most new laws, there still exist some questions about the concept and refinements to be made. Most attorneys are reluctant, and rightly so, to experiment with clients unless the case calls for it. Therefore, most new corporations are not formed as closed corporations but rather along the lines set out in this chapter. It is more likely that in the years ahead and as it develops, we will use the new close corporation for our clients.

Summary

It is important that a person who is new to the corporate form of business understand the how and why of the incorporation process. The first step, being the articles of incorporation, is in essence an application to the state of Texas to charter and begin the existence of the corporation. These articles of incorporation state the corporate name, period of duration, purpose, capitalization, address, initial directors, and the incorporators. Upon the articles of incorporation being approved, the corporate life begins.

Within a short period of time after the approval of the articles of incorporation, the organizational meeting of the corporation should be held. In addition to general organizational matters, the meeting will result in the election of officers and directors of the corporation and the issue of corporate stock to the owners of the corporation. Concurrent with the organizational meeting will be the preparation of the corporate book: a large notebook containing the corporation's minutes, bylaws, stock records, etc.

Relatively new to Texas is the concept of the close corporation, its purpose being to simplify the management of small corporations. Although not used nearly as frequently as the general business corporation, it should develop into a more favorable corporate form in the future.

Chapter 4

Operating Your Business as a Corporation

So your corporation is now formed. The articles of incorporation are filed, the organizational meeting held, and the corporate book along with the various documents included within it have been prepared by your attorney. Your accountant has you on the right road to proper record keeping and tax benefits. In general, the dust has settled over the incorporation process, and your business is operating. Now you must take specific steps to assure that the work done for you continues to benefit you. A corporation is much like a new plant or shrub. No matter how carefully it is chosen and planted, if it is not cared for, it will probably die. You must continue to care for the corporation to assure continued enjoyment of its benefits.

The reality, simply stated, is that many people spend a great deal of time and money having their business incorporated or perhaps incorporating themselves, but once the incorporation is completed, they forget about it. Our system of business is such that your accountant must file tax returns for you every year, but this requirement does not assure you that your corporation is an up-to-date, going concern. Usually, you find out there is a problem when one of two things happen, and both are bad. One, a person sues you and is able to "pierce the corporate veil," and you do not have the limited liability protection previously discussed. Or two, you are audited by the Internal Revenue Service and they are able to disallow your corporate tax benefits.

Fortunately, the basic reason why these misfortunes happen is known, and there is a remedy for them. The remedy is plainly stated: you must act and function as a corporation to continue the benefits of incorporation. You must use daily corporate formalities in your business operation and keep your personal affairs separate and apart from your business affairs. For example, your business checking account should always be separate from your personal checking account.

Return again to Article 2.31:

Art. 2.31. Board of Directors

    A. The business and affairs of a corporation shall be managed by a board of directors. Directors need not be residents of this State or shareholders of the corporation unless the articles of incorporation or bylaws so require. The articles of incorporation or bylaws may prescribe other qualifications for directors.

What the statue is saying is that whenever you have a significant or material transaction or event in the corporation, it should be approved by a resolution of the board of directors. To determine what is significant or material, use this test: If the event, whatever it may be, is not a normal and usual everyday activity in your business, it probably needs a decision by the board of directors. To get a decision, do you have to have a formal meeting of the board? No, not according to Article 9.10:

Art. 9.10. Actions Without a Meeting; Telephone Meetings

    A. Any action required by this Act to be taken at a meeting of the shareholders of a corporation, or any action which may be taken at a meeting of the shareholders, may be taken without a meeting if a consent in writing, setting forth the action so taken, shall be signed by all of the shareholders entitled to vote with respect to the subject matter thereof, and such consent shall have the same force and effect as a unanimous vote of shareholders, and may be stated as such in any articles or document filed with the Secretary of State.

B. Unless otherwise restricted by the articles of incorporation or bylaws, any action required or permitted to be taken at a meeting of the board of directors or any committee may be taken without a meeting if a consent in writing, setting forth the action so taken, is signed by all the members of the board of directors or committee, as the case may be. Such consent shall have the same force and effect as a unanimous vote at a meeting, and may be stated as such in any document or instrument filed with the Secretary of State.

C. Subject to the provisions required or permitted by this Act for notice of meetings, unless otherwise restricted by the articles of incorporation or bylaws, shareholders, members of the board of directors, or members of any committee designated by such board, may participate in and hold a meeting of such shareholders, board, or committee by means of conference telephone or similar communications equipment by means of which all persons participating in the meeting can hear each other, and participation in a meeting pursuant to this Section shall constitute presence in person at such meeting, except where a person participates in the meeting for the express purpose of objecting to the transaction of any business on the ground that the meeting is not lawfully called or convened.

Therefore, by simply having a written consent signed by all board members that states the action taken or decision made, you have fulfilled the necessary formalities of managing the corporation by the board of directors. In addition, the statute permits a meeting by telephone if not all directors are available in one place for a meeting.

Figure 4-1 is a form you might use to record the consent of directors to an action. You might simply copy it, reproduce it, complete it, and have all directors sign it. If you have any indication that an action is a significant or material decision being made by the corporation, use the form. It is far better to use it when not necessary than to miss having a written record of an important corporate decision. If you can establish this habit of documenting corporate activities, you will most likely avoid any threats to a loss of corporate status.

**Unanimous Consent to Corporate Action
Without a Board of Directors Meeting**

We, the undersigned being all of the Directors of *Burns & Green Home Care, Inc.* pursuant to Article 9.10 of the Texas Business Corporation Act, do hereby unanimously consent to the following corporate action being taken and direct that the officers of the corporation take such action:

That the corporation purchase for the use of its officers and employees a 1984 Chevrolet Blazer Pickup Truck from Alpha Chevrolet, Houston, Texas, for the price of $10,000.00. The officers may enter into such contracts and financing as is necessary to purchase such truck.

The above action is hereby ratified and approved this ____ day of _____, 19____.

_____
Benjamin Burns, Director

_____
Robert Green, Director

Figure 4-1. A consent form such as this permits a corporate decision to be made without having to convene a formal meeting of the board of directors.

During the year you can prepare these consents and then let your attorney review them, perhaps at the end of each year when you have your annual meeting. But use of this form does not eliminate the need of calling on your attorney for complicated or complex corporate transactions. This form is simply a method of following the corporate formalities of decision making and recording transactions. Document these decisions as shown, and at year's end you can smile at your attorney, who will smile back.

One more thing (there is always one more thing), the annual meeting of shareholders. Article 2.24 provides as follows:

Art. 2.24. Meetings of Shareholders
   A. Meetings of Shareholders may be held at such place within or without this State as may be stated in or fixed in accordance with the bylaws. If no other place is so stated or fixed, meetings shall be held at the registered office of the corporation.
   B. An annual meeting of the shareholders shall be held at such time as may be stated in or fixed in accordance with the bylaws. If the annual meeting is not held within any 13-month period, any court of competent jurisdiction in the county in which the principal office of the corporation is located may, on the application of any shareholder, summarily order a meeting to be held. Failure to hold the annual meeting at the designated time shall not work a dissolution of the corporation.
   C. Special meetings of the shareholders may be called by the president, the board of directors, the holders of not less than one-tenth of all the shares entitled to vote at the meetings, or such other persons as may be authorized in the articles of incorporation or the bylaws.

Once a year, at such time as provided in your bylaws, you need to hold a joint meeting of shareholders and directors. This can be your once-a-year basic "housekeeping" meeting for the corporation. Generally, each shareholder has one vote for each share of stock owned. At the meeting you can elect or reelect new officers and directors and construct a written record of the past year's activities for the corporation. Article 2.25 provides for notice of such meeting by shareholders:

Art. 2.25. Notice of Shareholders' Meetings
  A. Written or printed notice stating the place, day and hour of the meeting and, in case of a special meeting, the purpose or purposes for which the meeting is called, shall be delivered not less than ten (10) nor more than fifty (50) days before the date of the meeting, either personally or by mail, by or at the direction of the president, the secretary, or the officer or person calling the meeting, to each shareholder of record entitled to vote at such meeting. If mailed, such notice shall be deemed to be delivered when deposited in the United States mail addressed to the shareholder at his address as it appears on the stock transfer books of the corporation, with postage thereon prepaid.

In large corporations this notice is a routine matter. In smaller corporations the stockholders usually waive notice, as illustrated in Figure 4-2. The waiver should be signed and placed with the minutes of the meeting.

The minutes of the regular annual meeting of shareholders and directors may be prepared either before or after the annual meeting for small corporations, and Figure 4-3 is an example of the minutes for such a meeting.

**Waiver of Notice
Regular Joint Meeting of Shareholders and Directors of
Burns & Green Home Care, Inc.**

I, the undersigned, being a shareholder and/or director of the above corporation, do hereby waive having to receive notice of the regular joint meeting of shareholders and directors of the corporation and do consent that said meeting may be held at _____, Texas on _____, 19___, at the hour of ___.M., and that all necessary business may be conducted at that time.

    Dated _____, 19___

_____
Name

Figure 4-2. Stockholders of relatively small corporations can waive notice of stockholders' meetings with a form such as this.

**Minutes of a Joint Meeting of
The Shareholders and Directors of
*Burns & Green Home Care, Inc.***

    The joint annual meeting of the shareholders and directors of Burns & Green Home Care, Inc., a Texas corporation, was held at 1200 Hunt Drive, Houston, Texas on _____, 19___, at the hour of ___.M. The purpose of the meeting was to elect directors and officers, report on the corporation's affairs during the past year, and to consider any other business necessary. Present at the meeting were all the stockholders and directors of the corporation and it was declared that the meeting was lawfully

Figure 4-3. Keeping minutes of annual directors/shareholders meetings can be of great help in maintaining your business's corporate status.

Figure 4-3. (Continued on next page.)

convened. Attached to the minutes of the meeting was a waiver for any shareholders or directors unable to attend the meeting. The president of the corporation, Mr. Benjamin Burns, called the meeting to order and presided as chairman. The secretary of the corporation, Mr. Robert Green, presided as secretary of the meeting.

Prior Minutes Approved

The reading of the minutes of the last meeting of shareholders and directors was dispensed with without objection and on motion made, seconded, and carried, the minutes were approved as written.

A Report on the Affairs of the Corporation

The president of the corporation then rendered his report of the affairs of the corporation during the past year including the actions taken by the board of directors of the corporation in its management of the corporation. On motion made, seconded, and carried, these activities were ratified and approved by the shareholders.

Election of the Board of Directors

Nominations were then taken for the board of directors of the corporation to serve until their successors are elected. Nominated were Benjamin Burns and Robert Green. No further nominations being made, nominations were closed and the above persons were unanimously elected directors.

Election of Officers of the Corporation

The chairman then called for nominations for officers of the corporation. The following persons were nominated for the office as shown:

Benjamin Burns—President
Robert Green   —Secretary

Figure 4-3. (Continued on next page.)

No further nominations being made, nominations were closed and the above persons were unanimously elected to the office for which they were nominated.

Adjournment

There being no further business brought before the meeting, upon motion made, seconded, and carried, the meeting was hereby declared to be adjourned.

Dated and approved _____, 19__.

_____
Benjamin Burns, Chairman

_____
Robert Green, Secretary

Figure 4-3. Continued.

Summary

The fact that the initial incorporation has been completed does not mean that you can then forget about the corporate form of business and continue to operate your business as you have in the past. Instead you must continue to act and function as an incorporated business in order to benefit from this form. Since the corporation is managed by the board of directors, then this body must approve major and material events for the corporation. This approval may take place in a formal meeting or without a meeting as long as a written consent of the directors is obtained.

At least once each year there should take place a combined meeting of the directors and shareholders of the corporate. Among the things taking place at this meeting will be the approval of corporate actions taken during the year and the election of directors and officers for the coming year.

Thus, if you can form the habit of making your corporation decisions and managing the corporation through the board of directors; keeping written minutes of your director consents and year-end joint shareholders and directors meetings; and keeping the affairs and finances of the corporation separate and apart from your own personal affairs and finances; you will find your corporation running smoothly and correctly. Those who assist you with it will comment on your astute and intelligent business manner.

Chapter 5

Corporate Financing and Accounting

Basic accounting is simple and logical. What makes accounting easy to understand is that it is all based upon a simple formula:

$$Assets = Liabilities + Capital$$
$$or$$
$$Liabilities = Assets - Capital$$
$$or$$
$$Capital = Assets - Liabilities$$

First, some basic terminology:

Assets means things owned by a business that have value to the business.

Liabilities means claims upon these assets by persons outside the business; that is, people you owe money to, your creditors.

Capital means the owners' claim upon the business assets.

Back once more to Burns & Green Home Care, Inc. The corporation's list of assets, might read as follows:

Assets

Cash	$ 1,620.00
Tools	500.00
Truck	10,000.00
Total	$12,120.00

Assuming that the truck is financed and the company owes $8,000.00 to the finance company, then a liability is recorded:

Liability

Truck loan	$8,000.00

Therefore, according to the accounting formula, Capital = Assets − Liabilities:

Capital = $12,120.00 minus $8,000.00
Capital = $4,120.00

Knowing the assets, liabilities, and capital, you can then prepare one of the basic financial statements, the balance sheet.

Burns & Green Home Care, Inc.
Balance Sheet for Year Ended December 31, 1984

Assets

Cash	$1,620.00
Tools	500.00
Truck	10,000.00
Total Assets	$12,120.00

Liabilities

Note on truck	$8,000.00

Capital

Owners' capital	$4,120.00
Total Liabilities and Capital	$12,120.00

Ever wonder why a balance sheet balances? Because the total assets of a company are offset by two claims, those of creditors and those of owners. Therefore, when you have a balance sheet prepared for your company or read a balance sheet for another company, what you see is a picture of all the assets of the company balanced on the other side by its liabilities and capital. Why is this picture useful to you? Because it clearly shows what your claim (owner's claim) upon the business is in relation to the claims of people the business owes money to. In the event you desire to apply for a bank loan, the bank would like to see a balance sheet for your business. Of course, as your business operates, the assets, liabilities, and capital will change as a result of these operations. Most businesses prepare a balance sheet at the end of every year. By comparing several years' balance sheets, you have some idea of how successful the business has been.

The second basic financial statement is called the income statement, or as some call it, the profit and loss statement. Assume that the company completes several home building jobs this year. The total contract price of the jobs is $85,000.00. At the end of the year the company reviews its own costs of completing the jobs as follows:

Material (lumber, appliances, etc.)	$36,500.00
Labor (including subcontractors)	23,000.00
Miscellaneous expenses (including salary)	24,400.00
Total expenses	$83,900.00

The income statement is based on the following formula:
Revenues (what the company charges)
    − expenses (company costs) = income

The income statement might read as follows:

Burns & Green Home Care, Inc.
Income Statement
For Year Ended December 31, 1984

Revenue		$85,000.00
Less: Expenses—Material	$36,500.00	
—Labor	23,000.00	
—Operating expenses	24,400.00	83,900.00
Net income		$ 1,100.00

Therefore, the income statement shows how the revenue during the year compared to the expenses for that year. If there is more revenue than expense, the result is net income. If expenses are greater than revenues (not unusual in a starting business), there is a loss. If you are a business person, like it or not, these two statements become a part of your life. Fortunately, although they can become much more complex than shown here, the principle is the same. The balance sheet is a report on the status of your assets, liabilities, and capital as of the end of the year, and the income statement is a comparison of revenues and expenses to determine your yearly net income or net loss.

There is a third statement that may be prepared separately or as a part of the balance sheet. Once more some basic terminology:

Capital stock means the amount of investment you have placed in the company.

Retained earnings means income the corporation has had which has been retained within the company and not taken out of the corporation by the stockholders. This income is frequently and somewhat incorrectly termed *earned surplus* by attorneys.

This third statement reflects how the retained earnings of the corporation have changed within the past year. Your corporation's capital is composed of both the capital stock and the retained earnings you may have. A retained earnings statement for a corporation may look like this:

Burns & Green Home Care, Inc.
Retained Earnings Statement
For Year Ended December 31, 1984

Retained Earnings January 1,1984	$2,020.00
Add: Income for year 1984	1,100.00
Deduct: Dividends for the year	- 0 -
Retained Earnings December 31, 1984	$3,120.00

Your total capital in the corporation is your initial investment of $1,000.00 plus your retained earnings of $3,120.00 for a total of $4,120.00.

How do you get the information to prepare these statements? There are two fundamental jobs that your accountant should do. The first is to collect and arrange the information necessary to prepare these statements at year end. The second job is to evaluate the information from a tax standpoint and prepare your tax return.

Collecting Information

How the information is collected by the accountant on a daily basis will vary greatly from company to company.

Some companies, especially those without their own book-keepers, will let their accountant do everything for them. They just bring him their invoices, receipts, checks, etc. at the end of every month, and the business owner will have little involvement in the actual accounting. Other businesses have the accountant devise for them, or will devise for themselves, a system to collect the business accounting data, such as revenues and expenses, and then provide the accountant with the accumulated information at specific times during the year. Visit with the accountant, and look at your business and the resources available to you, and then decide how to collect the needed information. As a minimum, you will need a general ledger, a general journal, and a check writing system. Many accountants suggest for their clients one of the commercially available pegboard or one-write systems. These are relatively inexpensive accounting systems that will be of great assistance to you in collecting accounting data. But more important than anything, see your accountant at the beginning of your business, not at some point down the road. Your accountant may have an office full of computers, calculators, and coffee makers, but he does not have a time machine for returning to the past to retrieve information.

Evaluating Information for Tax Purposes

Generally, the accountant who has taken care of your accounting matters during the year is the most qualified person to prepare your federal corporate income tax return. When you employ an accountant to perform your routine accounting, confirm that he or she will also be available to complete your tax return. Having a qualified accountant prepare your tax return, both business and personal, will benefit you in three ways. First, you have a high assurance that the return has been correctly completed. Second, when the accountant examines the information you have provided to prepare the return, he can offer suggestions on improving your record-keeping system and new changes in the tax law that may influence your tax planning. Third, it is a fact of life that taxpayers are audited. In that event, you can imagine that there will be some comfort in knowing you will be represented at that audit by your accountant. At least he speaks the same language as the I.R.S. Read and learn as much as you can about the taxation of corporations, and let the preparation of your tax return be a joint undertaking between you and your accountant.

How Long Do You Keep Records?

Some businesses follow the "warehouse" theory of record keeping. They keep every piece of paper generated in the business until it fills a warehouse; then they throw everything away and start over. Your greatest need for records will be for a period up to six years after they are created. The Internal Revenue Service has three years to assess a tax based on a filed return and six years if a tax deficiency is a substantial omission from your return. Taking into consideration all the things that may happen to require you to produce accounting records, keep your records for fifteen years. After that, throw them away.

Cash Flow

A positive cash flow gives life to your business. It is the inflow of cash from revenue and the outflow for expenses. A positive cash flow indicates that you have more cash flowing in than is flowing out in the form of expenses. Thus, you are operating at a profit. You can operate with a negative cash flow for a short time, but over the long haul it must be positive. You may have a fine looking balance sheet and acceptable income statement, but if the positive cash flow is not there, you are in a critical situation.

Do you ever hear business people say, "Where did the money go?" A cash flow statement is very simple to make and will tell you where all that cash went. A simple format for a cash flow statement would be as follows:

Burns & Green Home Care, Inc.
Statement of Cash Flow
for December, 1984

Beginning balance of cash (checkbook balance 12/1)		$1,220
Sources of cash (deposit slips from bank)		
1. Payment on White kitchen job	$12,000	
Uses of cash (from checks written)		
1. Barton Lumber Co.	$6,500	
2. Sam Owens-Subcontractor	3,000	
3. Dallas Kitchen Supply	600	
4. Salaries	1,500	11,600
Excess of sources over uses of cash		$ 400
Ending cash balance 12/31/84		$1,620

By preparing this simple statement every month, you can monitor the inflow and outflow of cash within your business. Because other financial statements may be prepared only at the end of the year or perhaps every three months, this cash flow statement can be your best method of knowing how your business is doing.

Capital for Your Business

If you incorporate an existing business, the question of capital to operate your new corporation is probably not difficult. You will simply take the assets and liabilities from your old business and transfer them to the new one. Your credit is already established; and if you find a need for more cash, you will probably borrow it or invest some of your personal savings in the corporation.

A new business may have more challenges to meet in this area. Usually, the person or persons with the idea for a new business does not have enough money to finance it. There are basically two options available to raise capital:

1. Borrow money, thereby incurring debt for the corporation.
2. Sell ownership in the corporation in the form of stock.

Since the financial situation of each new corporation may differ greatly, it is difficult to offer guidance and direction in this area. Here is a checklist of some of the advantages and disadvantages of these two methods of raising capital.

Borrowing Money

☐ *Advantages*

1. Compared to raising money by selling stock, it is relatively simple in operation; and the money is available to you in full.
2. Interest on the loan, like other expenses of doing business, is tax deductible.
3. The lender, not receiving stock in the corporation, does not have any element of ownership in it. Since he has no stock, he has no voting power.

☐ *Disadvantages*

1. Since this is a loan, the money must be paid back with interest. This has a negative effect on cash flow.

2. The lender may place restrictions on your operation and ask that the loan be secured, thereby tying up some asset of the corporation.

A word of caution would be in order here. If you loan personal funds to the corporation, make certain a formal written promissory note is executed by the corporation for the loan. The loan should bear interest at or near market rate and should be repaid to you exactly as the terms of the note dictate. What you want to avoid is the loan being considered an additional investment into the corporation by the owner. If such would be the case, when the corporation repaid the loan, it could be considered a dividend and be taxable to you as income rather than repayment of a loan.

Selling Stock

☐ *Advantages*

1. The cash received in return for the stock is a permanent investment into the corporation.
2. The cash invested earns no interest and does not have to be repaid like a loan.

☐ *Disadvantages*

1. The person investing the cash becomes a part owner in the business and can enter into the decision-making process.
2. Investors expect some type of reward for having invested, such as dividends or employment with the company.

Thus, you can see that both methods of raising funds for a new corporation have pros and cons. You may use either or perhaps a combination of both. The exact method to be used is a decision made on a corporation-by-corporation basis by the owner and his attorney and accountant.

If you expect to sell stock in the corporation, you must be very careful about to whom and how the stock is sold. Since the early 1930s, there have been laws passed on the state and federal levels to protect investors from unscrupulous promoters of sometimes nonexistent corporations. Basically, these laws say that if you openly and publicly seek investors for your corporation, you must be registered with the Texas Securities Commissioner and perhaps with the Federal Securities Exchange Commission. The registration is highly complex, expensive, and for a small corporation is best avoided. Ideally, stockholders should be actively involved in the business. If you find it necessary to acquire capital by selling stock to non-active investors, be especially careful to avoid any public advertisement or solicitation for investors and sell only to such investors who reside in Texas. Your attorney should outline safeguards to follow with non-active investors.

Dividends or Salary: How Do You Get the Money Out of the Corporation?

Very carefully. It is most important that you keep separate the corporation finances and your own personal finances. Two separate bank accounts are especially important. Let us assume that your corporation is very successful and you now need to draw money out of the corporation for your personal needs.

Two methods are available to do this. First you may declare a dividend and take the money out as a corporate dividend. This is not, however, a good method of cash withdrawal because the money taken out as a dividend is taxed twice: once when the corporation made the money and again when the money is paid to you. A better method of cash withdrawal is to take a salary from the corporation. Granted the money is taxable to you when you receive it, but the corporation may deduct this as a salary expense from its own tax return. To use this method, simply decide what amount of salary the corporation can pay you and adopt this amount as a salary. The salary adopted should be approved by resolution either in your organizational meeting or by using a consent to act without meeting as discussed in the last chapter. The resolution might be worded as follows:

"Salary of Officers. It is resolved that the president of the corporation, Benjamin Burns, shall be paid a monthly salary of $____ commencing on December 1, 1984, and to continue on a monthly basis as long as he shall serve as president of the corporation or until changed by the Board of Directors."

On occasion you will find that you have left in the corporation, during or at the end of the year, cash that you wish to withdraw from the corporation in excess of your normal salary. Before you withdraw the cash, you should adopt a resolution to pay a bonus to the officers. Such a resolution might read as follows:

"Bonus to Officers. It is resolved that due to the extra effort of the officers of the corporation and the profitable status of the operations of the corporation that a bonus of $____ shall be paid to the president and secretary of the corporation. Said bonus shall be paid immediately."

The purpose of passing resolutions for salary and bonus matters is to assure that these amounts were not taken as dividends and subject to double taxation.

Summary

Although corporate accounting and finance may become very complex for large corporations, its basic elements are logical and easy to understand. Accounting is based on the simple formula that the assets, or things of value in your business, are equal to the liabilities, what you owe, plus the capital, your investment in the business. From this equation can be prepared a basic financial statement known as the balance sheet. A second financial statement, the income statement, can be developed by deducting the expenses of your business from its revenues. A third statement, particular to corporations, is the retained earnings statement. It measures the increase or decrease of the capital in your business. A portion of your accountant's duties will be to gather the information necessary to prepare these statements and, in addition, a cash flow statement for your business. The second duty of your accountant will be to prepare the necessary tax returns for your business.

Financing your corporation may involve either borrowing the funds, selling stock or a combination of these methods. Both have advantages and disadvantages. Your accountant may also advise you on the most tax effective manner in which to remove money from the corporation. The end result of good accounting advice will be the preparation of meaningful financial statements and assistance in the determination of how your capital can be gathered and managed in the corporation.

Chapter 6

Taxes and Your Corporation

The key to understanding the taxation of a corporation lies in one important fact: The corporation is an entity unto itself. It is a legal body separate and apart from you the owner and is taxed as such. Actually, a number of different taxes affect the corporation in addition to the federal corporate income tax. These are sales tax, franchise tax, withholding tax, F.I.C.A. tax, and other miscellaneous taxes. However, the most "substantial" tax—the federal corporate income tax—can be planned for and minimized. Texas has no state individual or corporate income tax. In general, the taxes other than the corporate income tax are fairly standard and routine in their collection. A good accountant will handle these for you, and you will not be greatly concerned over them. Therefore, this chapter will focus on the federal corporate income tax and your own individual federal income tax.

First, an overview of the three basic forms of business and how their income is taxed.

Sole Proprietorship

As discussed in Chapter 1, the sole proprietorship is one person engaged in some business activity. Legally, there is no separation between the person and the business. Therefore, when it comes time to pay the taxes on the income of the business (your revenue less your expenses), these are placed on Schedule C of your individual tax return. The total income is then carried to your Form 1040 and added to any other income you may have. The result is that your business income is taxed along with your other income at your individual tax rate. It is simple in operation (simple relative to taxation in general), but this method may deny you some very advantageous tax benefits.

Partnerships

A partnership is two or more individuals conducting some business together. From a taxation standpoint, it has some characteristics found in both the sole proprietorship and the corporation. First, like a sole proprietorship, each partner's share of the income is placed on Schedule E of that partner's Form 1040 individual tax return. Thus, partnership income is taxed at the same individual tax rate as the partner's other income.

Secondly, like a corporation, the partnership itself must file its own separate tax return on IRS Form 1065. This is a moderately complex form also due on April 15 for partnerships that adopt the calendar year as their business year. However, since the actual taxation of the partnership income takes place on the individual partner's own Form 1040, the partnership tax return is an information-only return. In other words, the partnership itself does not pay the tax on the income. Here, too, you may not find some of the tax advantages characteristic of corporations.

Tax Planning and the Corporation

Since the corporation is a legal entity apart from its owners, it is taxed as such. It files its own tax return and pays its own taxes. Only when monies are transferred from the corporation to the stockholders either by dividend or salary does that stockholder show this income on a Form 1040 individual return.

Tax planning simply means planning a course of action that will minimize the amount of income tax that the corporation and perhaps the shareholder must pay. There are many alternatives and options available to the corporation and shareholders regarding how they may operate the corporation. This is where a knowledgeable accountant and attorney will be worth a great deal to you. They will assist you in placing into operation your best tax options. But keep two things in mind. One, you will pay some tax somewhere. You may be able to minimize it or delay it, but do not expect absolute miracles. Two, no one can predict the future. Changes in the tax laws, economy, and business in general may help or hinder what has been planned for you. You must be flexible and expect adjustments as you go along.

Tax Considerations When Organizing Your Corporation

When a new corporation is formed or an existing business is incorporated, there are several initial tax decisions and operations that must be executed. The following is a checklist of the ones most commonly found in small corporations.

Application for a New Employer's Identification Number

When a new business or an old business is incorporated, an application for a new employer's identification number should be filed on Form SS-4 with the Internal Revenue Service. Even if you have a number for an old existing business, you still need a new number. This number identifies your corporation to the Internal Revenue Service and will be used on all correspondence with them. In addition, the Texas comptroller requires the employer's identification number on its annual franchise tax return. Since the Internal Revenue Service takes several weeks to assign the number, your attorney or accountant should apply for the new number as soon as your certificate of incorporation has been filed. An example of a completed form SS-4 is shown in Figure 6-1.

Choice of Business Year

When you form your new corporation, you may choose what type of business year you desire to use. Some corporations choose the calendar year; their business year ends on December 31. Others, especially in seasonable industries, elect to have their year end at some other point during the calendar year. An important consideration here is the fact your accountant is very busy at the end of the calendar year. If you select a business year ending perhaps on June 30, your accountant will have more time to assist you and prepare your tax return. Your corporate tax return is due by the fifteenth day of the third month after your business year ends.

Selection of Subchapter S Status

There may be some instances where the normal method of income taxation for a corporation will create a tax disadvantage for the shareholders. Most often this occurs if the corporation has a loss from the year's operation. In a partnership or sole proprietorship, this loss could offset other income that the sole proprietor or partner may have and help

Form SS-4
(Rev. 9–82)
Department of the Treasury
Internal Revenue Service

Application for Employer Identification Number
(For use by employers and others as explained in the instructions.)
Please read the instructions before completing this form.
For Paperwork Reduction Act Notice, see page 2.

OMB No. 1545-0003   Expires 9-30-85

1 Name (True name and not trade name. If partnership, see page 4.)
Burns & Green Home Care, Inc.

2 Social security no., if sole proprietor
N.A.

3 Ending month of accounting year
December

4 Trade name, if any, of business (if different from item 1)
N.A.

5 General partner's name, if partnership; principal officer's name, if corporation; or grantor's name, if trust
Benjamin Burns, President

6 Address of principal place of business (Number and street)
1200 Hunt Street

7 Mailing address, if different
N.A.

8 City, State, and ZIP code
Houston, Texas 70001

9 County of principal business location
Harris

10 Type of organization
☐ Governmental ☐ Individual ☐ Trust ☐ Partnership ☒ Corporation
☐ Nonprofit organization ☐ Other (specify)

11 Date you acquired or started this business (Mo., day, year)
January 1, 1984

12 Reason for applying
☒ Started new business ☐ Purchased going business ☐ Other (specify)

13 First date you paid or will pay wages for this business (Mo., day, year)
January 31, 1984

14 Nature of principal business activity (See instructions on page 4.)
General Contractor for residential buildings

15 Do you operate more than one place of business?
☐ Yes ☒ No

16 Peak number of employees expected in next 12 months (If none, enter "0") ▲ Two (2)
Nonagricultural Agricultural Household

17 If nature of business is manufacturing, state principal product and raw material used.

18 To whom do you sell most of your products or services?
☐ Business establishments (wholesale) ☒ General public (retail) ☐ Other (specify)

19 Have you ever applied for an identification number for this or any other business? ☐ Yes ☒ No
If "Yes," enter name and trade name. Also enter approx. date, city, and State where you applied and previous number if known. ▲

Under penalties of perjury, I declare that I have examined this application, and to the best of my knowledge and belief it is true, correct, and complete.

Signature and Title ▶

Date ▶ 1/1/84

Telephone number (include area code)
(713) 111-1111

Please leave blank ▶ | Geo. | Ind. | Class | Size | Reas. for appl. | Part I

Figure 6-1. Once your certificate of incorporation has been filed, you should use IRS Form SS-4 to apply for a new employer's identification number.

lower that person's individual income tax. In a corporation, however, the loss cannot be taken personally by the shareholders; thus, it would really not benefit them. Subchapter S is a selection the corporate shareholders may make in order not to be taxed as a corporation, but instead as a partnership. Under this option, profits and losses will be divided between the shareholders, who will pay the income tax on any profits or deduct any losses on their own individual Form 1040. The selection of the Subchapter S status is made on Internal Revenue Service Form 2553, which must be filed within the first seventy-five days of the year you desire to be taxed as such. For a new corporation wanting to begin as a Subchapter S corporation, filing must take place within seventy-five days of whichever of the following occurs first: (1) when the corporation has shareholders, (2) when the corporation acquires assets, or (3) when the corporation begins to do business.

There are three important factors to be aware of when adopting the Subchapter S plan.

First, *this is just a tax election.* It does not affect your legal status as a corporation. Therefore, you still have your limitation of liability and most of the other legal advantages of incorporation. However, since your income is being taxed at your individual tax rates, you lose one of the basic tax advantages of incorporation. You cannot retain income within the corporation at the lower corporate tax rates. It is taxed at your personal rate.

Second, the primary reason to elect Subchapter S treatment is the *anticipation of losses for the corporation.* Since the election must be made before or in the very early part of the loss year, you must use your best planning ability to anticipate a loss year ahead.

Third, if you elect to be a Subchapter S corporation, *you are not locked in to that election forever.* If you determine that the election is no longer to your benefit, you may revoke it and return to being taxed as a regular corporation. The revocation must be filed by the fifteenth day of the third month for the business year in which it will be effective. The revocation must be agreed to by shareholders holding at least 50% of the corporation stock.

Although Subchapter S may seem relatively simple as it has been explained, in its actual application, it can be very complex. The final decision to elect to be a Subchapter S corporation should be made by a person knowledgeable in this area of taxation.

Transfer of Assets Into the Corporation

For a new business or an existing business being incorporated, the transfer of assets into the corporation in return for corporate stock must be carefully structured. Normally, an exchange of an asset for stock would be a taxable transaction. However, there is an exception in Section 351 of the Internal Revenue Code, wherein assets transferred to the corporation are a tax-free exchange where only the corporation's stock is received in return for the assets and the person transferring assets to the corporation receives a controlling interest in the corporation. Generally, an existing business will transfer into the new corporation all of its business assets, including its accounts payable and accounts receivable. However, in most instances it may be more effective for tax purposes and safer not to transfer buildings and equipment to the corporation, but instead to retain them as an individual and lease them to the new corporation. In the event of a later sale of the buildings or equipment, you may elect a capital gains treatment resulting in a lower tax that might not be available if these assets were owned by the corporation. Additionally, in the event of a lawsuit the assets might be subject to being taken if they are held in the corporate name. If you hold them as an individual, they would be protected from a judgment against the corporation.

Tax Considerations When Operating
Your Corporation

After the establishment of the new corporation, the ordinary and necessary expenses of conducting business are deductible as business expenses. These expenses must be directly connected with your business and be reasonable in amount.

For the purpose of discussion, these tax deductible expenses may be divided into two groups. In the first group are those expenses that are plainly associated with the activity of the corporation, usually reasonable in amount, and as a rule not contested by the Internal Revenue Service. These expenses are items such as rent; utilities (including electricity, water, and telephone); depreciation; salaries to non-related, non-stockholder employees; and other routine business expenses. Since these costs are rarely contested by the Internal Revenue Service, they deserve no further comment here.

The second group would be those expenses that lie somewhere between being purely business and being personal. These are commonly termed "fringe benefits" and imply that an employee is being furnished without charge a benefit that, but for the employment status with the business, he would normally have to pay for himself. The questions on these expenses usually relate to one or more of the following:

- Vehicles and commuting
- Entertainment expenses
- Travel expenses
- Dues to organizations
- Educational expenses
- Insurance (life and accident)
- Retirement plans
- Death benefits
- Loans to officers

Vehicles and Commuting

One of the first questions asked by a new corporation owner usually relates to vehicles. Since the cost of operation of even an economy car has risen to high levels, owners are interested in the maximum amounts of fringe benefits they can receive in this area. Generally, the cost of commuting to and from work is not deductible. Once you arrive at work, if you then travel to several work sites during the day, travel is a deductible expense. This is the case no matter what business form you operate under. Since only these non-commuting trips are deductible as business expenses, it makes no real difference who owns the vehicle. If the owner of the corporation uses a personal vehicle in the business of the corporation, then he should be reimbursed for vehicle expense, and this reimbursement is a deductible expense to the corporation. If the corporation owns the vehicle, then it will pay the normal expenses of operation. Most often in the new corporation, the corporation will purchase a vehicle in its name and at its expense for the use of the owner of the corporation—well and good as long as it is only used in corporate business. If the owner wants to use it for personal use, then the best practice is to have the owner reimburse the corporation for that personal use.

Additionally, it may be advantageous for the corporation to investigate the leasing of vehicles. Since the lease payments are fully deductible to the corporation, and only a small amount of cash is required to begin the lease, it may become a much larger tax advantage to you to lease rather than purchase a vehicle.

Entertainment and Travel Expenses

Again, these are business expenses that are deductible whether you are a sole proprietorship, a partnership, or a corporation. However, these are areas in which there has been so much controversy that a great deal of substantiation is necessary to support them in the event of an audit. Not only must you support the amounts involved, you must support the reason for the entertainment or travel.

Dues to Organizations

Dues to clubs, such as country clubs and civic organizations, are deductible if they meet two criteria. Was the club joined for business reasons, and is more than 50% of the use of the club for business reasons? Again, you must have the records to support such a deduction. If you meet the 50% test, then you may deduct the expense personally or you may have your corporation deduct a pro rata amount of the dues based on your business use as compared to your personal use.

Educational Expenses

Can your corporation send your children to college and deduct the expense? No. However, it can pay for or reimburse you for taking an educational program that improves your talents or skills in your business. However, you cannot deduct the cost of education that qualifies you for a new profession or trade.

Preferred Deductions for the Corporation

Here is where being a corporation begins to help you. To this point we have talked about deductions that are common to all forms of business. If you can support them and they are allowed, you can use them in any form of business. Now we will consider items that are specially treated in the corporate form of business.

☐ *Health and Accident Insurance.* This is one of the corporation's advantages, because the corporation may provide such coverage for its employees, and any amount received by them under the plan is not taxable as compensation. In addition, the premium payment for such plans is deductible as an expense of the corporation. As a comparison, if you are self-employed, these premium payments must be paid by you personally and are not deductible for most people in higher tax brackets. The corporation may also adopt a medical reimbursement plan that pays all medical expenses not covered by your insurance, such as a deductible amount, dental, etc.

☐ *Life Insurance.* Another fringe benefit especially attractive to the corporate form of business is *life* or *disability insurance.* Not only are the proceeds of the policy tax-exempt, the premiums are not taxable to the employee and are a deduction for the corporation. Once more, if you were a sole proprietor, you would not be able to deduct these premiums.

☐ *Death Benefits.* The corporation may pay to the beneficiary of a deceased employee an amount up to $5,000.00, which is non-taxable to his heirs and a deduction for the corporation.

☐ *Disability Insurance.* This is also a deduction to the corporation, but not to you if you are self-employed or in a partnership. Although many businesses carry health, life, and accident insurance, few carry a disability insurance policy. What happens if you should become disabled? Perhaps no one else can step in and operate the business as you would desire, but a disability insurance policy can provide income to support you in the event of a disability and help pay the overhead of your business.

Loans to Shareholders

This is a corporate fringe benefit you might well avoid. It is included here because some business owners consider it a fringe benefit. As noted earlier, corporate tax rates are lower by far than personal rates. Thus, money the corporation earns may build up in the corporation due to these lower rates. This is a great advantage for you, especially if you are spending this income on new capital items for the corporation. You are buying the corporate assets with dollars taxed at a lower rate than your own personal rate. However, if the corporation is not spending the money and you suddenly need personal cash, you may be tempted to borrow from the corporation. Even if this is a true legitimate loan, this area is presently so unsettled that you run a material risk the Internal Revenue Service will consider a loan to be a dividend, which is taxable income. If you find you must borrow money from your corporation, make sure that the loan is handled exactly the same as if you had borrowed the money from your bank. A written note should be signed, secured if possible, bear a market rate of interest, and be repaid as the note terms set out.

Retirement Plans

This is one of the corporate tax benefits that is in the process of being equalized with the other forms of business, including partnerships and sole proprietorships. At one time this was one of the major tax benefits of incorporation. It is still a major benefit, but now more equally available to other forms of business. Contributions to a retirement plan are tax deductions to the corporations, and not taxable to the employee as to the contribution or the interest earned on the contribution. A plan of this type is beneficial to a corporation that finds it has made more money than the owners need to remove in salary. The extra money may be shifted to a retirement plan and then withdrawn from the plan upon the owner's retirement, very possibly when he is in a lower tax bracket.

There are several different types of retirement plans to choose from. The choice depends a great deal upon the type of business and its degree of profitability. By all means, seek the assistance of a person knowledgeable in this particular field and do a great deal of investigation before adopting a particular plan. You can usually get a referral to such a professional from your attorney, accountant, insurance advisor, or stockbroker. Talk to more than one of these retirement plan advisors and determine if there is an agreement among them regarding what your best plan may be.

Sale of Your Corporation

Perhaps you have the idea of someday selling your business and retiring. You will usually find that you have a better tax treatment of the profit on your sale if you sell a corporation rather than a sole proprietorship. If you sell a corporation, your profits will be taxed on a capital gains basis. If you sell a sole proprietorship, you will generally be taxed partly on a capital gains basis and partly on an ordinary gains basis. In some instances, people incorporate their business for no other reason than to sell it in the future.

The subject of taxes is so broad that many books could be, and have been, written on the subject. The purpose of this chapter is not to tell you how to complete a corporate tax return or become an expert in the field but rather to tell you how a corporation is taxed, what initial tax decisions need to be made, and to point out some of the tax benefits available to a routinely operating corporation. The best advice that can be given on the subject of taxes is to keep good records and use the services of a good accountant or attorney. Such professionals will usually save you far more money than their fees.

Summary

Corporations, due to their separate legal identity, are taxed very differently than sole proprietorships or partnerships. When your corporation is first formed, there are several initial tax decisions that must be made, among them the choice of a business year, possible Sub-chapter S election, and the question of what assets will be transferred into the corporation. Once a corporation has begun to operate, you may begin to maximize the benefits that have now become available to you.

Chapter 7

Professional Corporations and Associations

Professional corporations and associations are a corporate form of business available to people who until a few years ago could not incorporate at all. These are persons who are licensed to practice what some would term "the professions"—physicians, attorneys, dentists, veterinarians, and accountants, among others. For some years there was a hesitation on the part of the legislature to allow these individuals to incorporate. This reluctance may have been because the limitation of liability is an attribute of the corporate form of business and the legislature did not want these professionals to avoid the liabilities of their professional acts. Finally, with the passage of the Texas Professional Corporation Act and the Texas Professional Association Act, Article 1528e and f respectively of the Revised Civil Statutes of Texas, professionals were allowed to incorporate, but without the limitation of liability, which is common to the business corporation. The Professional Corporation Act applies to all of the above named professionals with the exception of physicians. Physicians are governed under the Professional Association Act.

Other than the absence of limitation of liability, there are very few differences between professional corporations and associations and business corporations. In fact the Business Corporation Act applies to the professional corporations and associations unless there is a conflict between the acts. In the event of a conflict, the Professional Act governs.

Formation of the Professional Corporation or Association

The procedure of incorporation of the professional corporation or association does not differ greatly from the business corporation. The articles of incorporation are prepared and state specifically the one and only purpose of the corporation and set out the names of the licensed shareholders. The articles are filed in the same manner as for a business corporation. Once the articles are filed, the corporate book is prepared and the organizational meeting conducted. Thereafter, most of the actions discussed in the remainder of this book are equally applicable to the professional corporation or association. Figure 7-1 is a checklist formerly used by the office of the secretary of state to check newly submitted articles of incorporation of professional corporations, and Figure 7-2 is its counterpart for associations.

The more significant differences between the business corporation and the professional corporation or association are as follows:

1. Each incorporator, director, officer, and shareholder must be licensed to render the professional service for which the professional corporation or association was formed. Therefore, persons licensed in different professions may not form one professional corporation.

Date   Name

Processed by: _____

☐ Need $_____   Refund $_____

☐ Is the name available?   _____

☐ Is the name identical in Heading and Article I?   _____

☐ Is *Company, Corporation, Incorporated, Professional Corporation* or abbreviation of any of these words included in title? (P.C. abbreviation can be used)   _____

☐ Is the term of existence set out?   _____

☐ Is the post office address of its principal office and initial registered office in Texas given? (building or street address)   _____

☐ Is the initial registered agent named? (Must be at the same address as registered office)   _____

☐ Are there at least *two* initial directors? Are their addresses shown? (city and state)   _____

☐ Is there at least *one* incorporator? Is(Are) the address(es) shown? (city and state)   _____

☐ Are the shareholders listed? Are their addresses shown? (city and state)   _____

☐ Are the directors, shareholders, and incorporators licensed in this State to render the professional service of the corporation?   _____

☐ Did all the incorporators sign?   _____

☐ Did all the incorporators verify?   _____

☐ Do we have duplicate originals of the articles?   _____

☐ Is duplicate signed and verified with notary seal, signature, and date?   _____

Lawyer's Comments:

Figure 7-1. This checklist was formerly used by the office of the secretary of state to check newly submitted articles of incorporation of professional corporations.

Need $_____   Refund $_____   Correct _____

☐ Is the name available?   _____

☐ Is the name identical in Heading and Article I?   _____

☐ Is *Associated, Association, Professional Association, Associates,* or the abbreviation *Assoc.* or
P.A. included in the title?   _____

☐ Is the term of existence set out? Perpetual must
include "except last surviving member" or sub-
ject to Section 8 of Article 1528F, VATS.   _____

☐ Is there a statement that no member of a P.A.
shall have the power to dissolve the association
by his independent act of any kind?   _____

☐ Is the address of the association in Texas given?   _____

☐ Is the registered office and registered agent at
the same address stated?   _____

☐ Are each of the original members or shareholders licensed to perform the type of professional
service of the association? (M.D. or Osteopath)   _____

☐ Is the number of directors (one or more) and their
addresses (at least city and state) included?   _____

☐ Are the names and addresses of the original
members given? (city and state)   _____

☐ Did all the members sign and verify? (at least
one)   _____

☐ Is notary seal, signature, and date on the verifi-
cation?   _____

☐ Do we have duplicate originals of the applica-
tion?   _____

☐ Is the duplicate signed and verified with notary
seal, signature, and date?   _____

*Figure 7-2. This checklist was formerly used by the office of
the secretary of state to check newly submitted articles of incorporation of associations.*

2. The corporation must render only that one type of service for which it was formed and any normal types of support services necessary. This stipulation is in contrast to the business corporation, wherein under the general purpose clause a person might perform many unrelated services or business functions.
3. There may be a slight difference in corporate names. Professional corporations may use the normal indications of corporate status, such as "Inc." and "Corp.," or in lieu of these may use the initials "P.C." Professional associations must end their name with Professional Association, Associates, Associated, or P.A.
4. As previously indicated, there is no limitation of liability between the client or patient and the professional. Therefore, the professional, in the event of an error, will be liable personally in addition to his corporation or association.

Tax Benefits

Since there is no limitation of liability, aside from some minor benefits such as better organization, the major reason these professionals incorporate is for tax reasons. As a corporation or association, the professional may take advantage of the corporate tax benefits, some of which are unavailable to them as sole practitioners or partners.

Considering that these professionals are often in a very high tax bracket, any tax benefits available to them are very important. The tax benefits are those discussed in the tax chapter but are briefly the following:

□ *Profit Sharing and Pension Plans.* Even after a short period of operation, a professional corporation or association, and especially in the case of physicians and others in the medical arts, may find that cash beyond immediate needs is building up in the practice. This excess cash may be contributed to a retirement plan. These monies are not taxed as income and are a deduction to the corporation or association from its current year taxable income.

☐ *Death Benefits.* This includes life insurance and a $5,000 cash benefit from the corporation. The premiums on a life insurance policy with a face amount not exceeding $50,000 is a deduction to the corporation and not taken as income to the professional.

☐ *Insurance Benefits.* The corporation or association may provide health, accident, or disability insurance for the professional. Again, these are a business deduction to the practice and usually not included in the professional's net income.

Therefore, most professionals either have incorporated or are examining their financial status to determine if they will benefit from an incorporation. As with the normal business corporation, the tax benefits encourage many professional corporations and associations.

Summary

Relatively new in the corporate law is the incorporation of professional practices. This allows professionals such as accountants, attorneys, physicians, etc., to avail themselves of the benefits of the corporate form of business but without the limitation of liability. The basic procedure of incorporation for these individuals is very similar to that of the regular business corporation. However, some additional rules exist regarding who may be a shareholder, director, or officer of this type of corporation. The tax benefits of these corporations are also very much the same as those for the general business corporation.

Chapter 8

Nonprofit
Corporations

Because this book is directed to businesses, its readers' main interest will be in the general business corporation, professional corporation, or professional association. However, there does exist a form of nonprofit corporation in Texas. Nonprofit corporations are established and governed under Article 1396-1.01, Texas Civil Statutes, or the Nonprofit Corporation Act as it is known. As the name implies, they are created for some purpose other than producing a profit on their operations, and no part of their income can be distributed to their members, officers, or directors. However, some nonprofit corporations do generate a large amount of money and have many characteristics of a large business corporation.

Article 1396-2.01 allows a nonprofit corporation to be formed for a number of purposes including, but not limited to, charitable, benevolent, religious, eleemosynary (meaning supported by charity), patriotic, civic, missionary, educational, scientific, social, fraternal, athletic, aesthetic, agricultural, and horticultural organizations.

Reason to Incorporate

Why would a church, fire department, or civic group decide to incorporate? Aside from the benefits of having a definite legal status, the main reason is that of liability. In an unincorporated group, the members may be personally liable for debts and actions of the group. The effect of incorporation is that these members are not personally liable for the debts, liabilities, or obligations of the corporation. Thus, the incorporation helps to shelter the members from such liabilities. In addition, since a corporation, nonprofit or otherwise, does have an established legal form, it may provide for better management of the nonprofit group. Many unincorporated groups are loosely organized and poorly managed. Having to follow the management structure of the corporate form of business will usually provide for a better managed organization.

Procedure of Incorporation

The procedure of incorporation is generally the same as for a business corporation. The articles of incorporation are written and filed, the organizational meeting held, and the corporate book prepared. Shown in Figure 8-1 is the checklist formerly used by the secretary of state to approve articles of incorporation of a nonprofit corporation. In addition, the nonprofit corporation should seek an exemption from the state franchise tax on corporations and from federal income tax. The state comptroller of Texas determines whether the nonprofit corporation is qualified as a tax exempt corporation for the purpose of franchise tax. The controller usually requires a letter outlining the planned activities of the corporation, copies of any available brochures that may be printed about the corporation, and a two-year budget for a charitable

Date	Name

Processed by: _____

☐ Need $_____   Refund $_____

☐ No money, need filing fee of $ _____   _____

☐ Is the name available?   _____

☐ Is the name available with a letter?   _____

☐ Is the name identical in Heading and Article I?   _____

☐ Are all the incorporators at least 18 years of age and at least two citizens of Texas?   _____

☐ Is there a statement that the corporation is a nonprofit corporation?   _____

☐ Is the period of duration set out?   _____

☐ Is the post office address of its initial registered office in Texas given? (building or street address)   _____

☐ Are there at least *three* initial Directors or Trustees? Are their addresses shown? (at least city and state)   _____

☐ Are there at least *three* incorporators? Are their addresses shown? (at least city and state)   _____

☐ Did all incorporators verify?   _____

☐ Did all the incorporators sign?   _____

☐ Is the notary seal, signature, and date on verification?   _____

☐ Do we have duplicate originals of the Articles?   _____

☐ Is duplicate signed and verified with notary seal, signature, and date?   _____

☐ Part Four   _____

☐ Trustee   _____

☐ Lawyer's Comments:

Figure 8-1. This checklist was formerly used by the office of the secretary of state to approve articles of incorporation of a nonprofit corporation.

organization. The application for the exemption from federal income taxes is Form 1023 and is somewhat detailed in the information required. It should be completed and filed with the Internal Revenue Service.

Summary

The corporate form may be adopted by both profit and nonprofit groups. In general the method of formation and operation will be the same for both type entities. In addition to providing a limitation of liability, adoption of the corporate form of organization will usually result in better management practices in the organization.

Appendix A

Post-Incorporation Checklist

After your company is incorporated, and especially if it was previously a sole proprietorship or partnership, you should notify several other parties of your company's new status. The following is a checklist of parties you need to contact and the internal actions you will need to take:

- ☐ All letterhead, contracts, business cards, etc. should be reprinted to show the new corporate name. You may use a rubber stamp to imprint existing printed documents with the new corporate name.
- ☐ All advertising, signs, and telephone listings should be changed to the new corporate name.
- ☐ A new bank account should be opened in the new corporate name.
- ☐ A new employer's identification number should be applied for with the Internal Revenue Service.
- ☐ All insurance carriers should be informed of your new corporate status in writing, including life, health, accident, worker's compensation, errors and omissions, etc.

☐ All existing leases, contracts, loans, etc. should be transferred to the corporation and/or renegotiated in the corporate name when their existing terms expire.

☐ Your accountant should begin a new set of accounting records for the corporation and complete any tax returns or applications necessitated by the incorporation.

☐ You should contact the issuer of any licenses held by the former business to arrange their transfer to the corporation.

☐ You should discuss with your accountant, attorney, and insurance agent what additional benefits are now available for you as a corporation.

Appendix B

Sample of Corporate Bylaws

Bylaws of Burns & Green Home Care, Inc.

Article I—Registered Office and Agent

1.01 The registered office of the Corporation shall be located at *1200 Hunt Street, Houston*, Texas and the registered agent for the corporation shall be *Benjamin Burns*.

Article II—Annual Meetings of Shareholders

2.01 The annual meeting of the shareholders of the corporation shall be held each year on the *first* day of *February*. If this date shall fall on a legal holiday, then the annual meeting may be held on the next business day following the specified date.

2.02 The location for the annual meeting shall be at the registered office of the corporation or such other location as may be decided upon by the board of directors of the corporation.

2.03 Notice of the annual meeting shall be given in writing to each shareholder entitled to vote at said meeting at least 10 but not more than 50 days before the meeting. The notice shall state the place, date, and time of the meeting. Said notice may be delivered either by mail addressed to the shareholder at his mailing address according to the records of the corporation, or to the shareholder personally.

Article III—Special Meeting of Shareholders

3.01 Special meetings of shareholders for any purpose may be called at any time by the president of the corporation, the board of directors of the corporation, or by the shareholders of the corporation who hold at least one-tenth (¹/₁₀) of the total number of shares allowed to vote at the meeting.

3.02 Notice of a special meeting of the shareholders shall be given in the same manner as set forth in Article 2.03 of these bylaws.

Article IV—Voting of Stock

4.01 Each outstanding share of stock that has voting power is entitled to one vote on each such matter to be decided upon at the shareholders' meeting. A shareholder may vote in person or by a proxy holder having a duly written and executed proxy.

4.02 A majority of the voting shares being present at the shareholders' meeting shall constitute a quorum for the transaction of business in a meeting. The affirmative vote of a majority of the shares at a meeting properly called and having a quorum present shall ratify the decision acted upon unless a greater number shall be required by statute.

4.03 In the election of directors for the corporation, each shareholder may have a number of votes equal to the number of directors being elected multiplied by the number of shares held by the shareholder.

4.04 Shareholders may take actions without a meeting by execution of a written consent to the action.

Article V—Directors of the Corporation

5.01 The affairs and decisions of the corporation shall be managed and made by the board of directors. These directors may in turn give authority to the officers of the corporation to transact general or special business for the corporation.

5.02 The corporation shall have a board of directors composed of *two* directors. The number of directors may be changed from time to time by amendment of these bylaws. The directors shall be elected at the annual meeting of the shareholders of the corporation and shall hold office until their successors are elected. A vacancy in the board of directors shall be filled by a majority vote of the remaining directors even though this may be less than a quorum of the board of directors and such directors elected shall fill the remaining term of the vacating directors.

5.03 A director or directors may be removed from office either with or without cause by a vote of the majority of the voting shares of the corporation.

Article VI—Meetings of the Board of Directors

6.01 The meetings of the board of directors may be held at such location, either within or without the state of Texas, as may be decided upon by the board of directors of the corporation.

6.02 The regular annual meeting of the board of directors shall be held either concurrently with or immediately after the annual meeting of the shareholders of the corporation. No notice of this meeting shall be necessary to the newly elected directors.

6.03 Special meetings of the board of directors for any purpose may be called at any time by the president, vice-president, or any director of the corporation. Written notice of the special meeting stating the time, date, location, and purpose of the special meeting shall be mailed or personally delivered to each director not less than five (5) days prior to the date set for the special meeting. Attendance of a director at a special or regular meeting shall constitute a waiver of notice of said meeting unless the attendance is to object to the transaction of any business due to the meeting not being lawfully called or convened.

6.04 A majority of the board of directors shall constitute a quorum to conduct business for the corporation and the act of a majority of the board of directors shall be an act of the board of directors unless a greater number shall be required by law.

6.05 Any action required to be taken by the board of directors in a meeting may be taken instead by a written consent executed by all of the directors of the corporation and shall have the same force and effect as if taken by the board of directors in a regular meeting.

6.06 At any meeting in which a quorum of the directors is present, the directors may adjourn said meeting and notice of the time and place of said reconvened meeting shall be given at the adjourned meeting.

6.07 The president of the corporation shall preside at the meetings of the board of directors. In the president's absence, the vice-president or a member of the board selected by the directors shall preside.

6.08 Members of the board of directors shall receive such compensation for their services and expenses as may be set by the board of directors by resolution.

Article VII—Officers of the Corporation

7.01 The officers of the corporation shall be elected by the board of directors and shall be a president and a secretary. At the discretion of the board of directors, other officers of the corporation may be elected including a vice-president, treasurer, and any other such officers that the board may desire. The board shall set the compensation and benefits of each officer.

7.02 The officers of the corporation shall hold office until their successors are elected and/or chosen and may be removed at any such time as may be determined by a majority vote of the board of directors. Any office becoming vacant shall be filled by the board of directors.

7.03 The president of the corporation shall be the chief officer of the corporation and shall preside at meetings of shareholders and board of directors. He shall be responsible to the board to see that their decisions are carried out and effected into the every day management of the corporation.

7.04 The vice-president of the corporation, if such shall be elected, shall perform the duties of the president in his absence.

7.05 The secretary of the corporation shall be in charge of the records of the corporation and shall be responsible for keeping written minutes of the shareholders' and directors' meetings. In addition, he shall be responsible for giving such notices of the meetings as may be required by these bylaws.

7.06 The treasurer of the corporation, if such shall be elected, shall be responsible for the funds of the corporation and keeping accurate records for the receipt and payment of such funds. In addition, he shall make such reports to the board of directors as may be required by said board.

7.07 In addition to the previously stated duties, the officers of the corporation shall have such powers and duties as are generally ascribed to their respective offices or as may be determined by the board of directors.

7.08 The board of directors may from time to time designate certain corporate officers to execute certain instruments and such execution pursuant to a resolution by the board of directors shall be binding upon the corporation.

Article VIII—Corporate Stock

8.01 Evidence of ownership by shareholders in the corporation shall be a certificate for shares of stock in the corporation. Such certificates shall only be issued when the stock has been fully paid for to the corporation. Each certificate shall be printed with the name of the corporation, a statement that the corporation has been organized within the state of Texas, the name of the shareholder, the number of shares represented by the certificate, and a statement of the par value of the stock or a statement that the stock has no par value. The certificates shall be signed by the president and secretary of the corporation.

8.02 In the event that a certificate shall have been lost or destroyed, then the board of directors may set such terms, conditions, and guarantees as it shall deem prudent and reasonable prior to the issuance of a new certificate.

8.03 Shares of stock in the corporation may be transferred by surrendering to the corporation a properly endorsed share certificate by the transferee of the stock. A new certificate shall then be issued to the new shareholder, the old certificate cancelled, and the transaction recorded on the stockholder's ledger of the corporation.

8.04 For the purpose of the determination of who shall be entitled to vote at a meeting of the shareholders of the corporation or receive a dividend from the corporation, the stock transfer books of the corporation shall be closed by the board of directors for a period not exceeding fifty (50) days prior to said meeting or the payment of said dividend.

Article IX—Fiscal Year

9.01 The fiscal year of the corporation shall begin on the *first* day of *January* of each year.

Article X—Amendment of Bylaws

10.01 The board of directors of the corporation shall have the power to amend, change, or repeal these bylaws at any regular or special meeting of the board of directors at which a quorum shall be present. The shareholders shall have the right to repeal or change any such action of the board of directors relating to a bylaw change.

Appendix C

Excerpts from Texas Business Corporation Act

Art. 2.02. General Powers

A. Subject to the provisions of Sections B and C of this Article, each corporation shall have power:

(1) To have perpetual succession by its corporate name unless a limited period of duration is stated in its articles of incorporation. Notwithstanding the articles of incorporation, the period of duration for any corporation incorporated before September 6, 1955 is perpetual if all fees and franchise taxes have been paid as provided by law.

(2) To sue and be sued, complain and defend, in its corporate name.

(3) To have a corporate seal which may be altered at pleasure, and to use the same by causing it, or a facsimile thereof, to be impressed on, affixed to, or in any manner reproduced upon instruments of any nature required to be executed by its proper officers.

(4) To purchase, receive, lease, or otherwise acquire, own, hold, improve, use and otherwise deal in and with, real or personal property, or any interest therein, wherever situated, as the purposes of the corporation shall require.

(5) To sell, convey, mortgage, pledge, lease, exchange, transfer and otherwise dispose of all or any part of its property and assets.

(6) To lend money to, and otherwise assist, its employees, officers, and directors if such a loan or assistance reasonably may be expected to benefit directly or indirectly, the lending or assisting corporation.

(7) To purchase, receive, subscribe for, or otherwise acquire, own, hold, vote, use, employ, mortgage, lend, pledge, sell or otherwise dispose of, and otherwise use and deal in and with, shares or other interests in, or obligations of, other domestic or foreign corporations, associations, partnerships, or individuals, or direct or indirect obligations of the United States or of any other government, state, territory, government district, or municipality, or of any instrumentality thereof.

(8) When permitted by the other provisions of this Act, to purchase or otherwise acquire its own bonds, debentures, or other evidences of its indebtedness or obligations, and, to purchase or otherwise acquire its own shares, and to redeem or purchase shares made redeemable by the provisions of its articles of incorporation.

(9) To make contracts and incur liabilities, borrow money at such rates of interest as the corporation may determine, issue its notes, bonds, and other obligations, and secure any of its obligations by mortgage or pledge of all or any of its property, franchises, and income.

(10) To lend money for its corporate purposes, invest and reinvest its funds, and take and hold real and personal property as security for the payment of funds so loaned or invested.

(11) To conduct its business, carry on its operations, and have offices and exercise the powers granted by this Act, within or without this state.

(12) To elect or appoint officers and agents of the corporation for such period of time as the corporation may determine, and define their duties and fix their compensation.

(13) To make and alter bylaws, not inconsistent with its articles of incorporation or with the laws of this state, for the administration and regulation of the affairs of the corporation.

(14) To make donations for the public welfare or for charitable, scientific, or educational purposes.

(15) To transact any lawful business which the board of directors shall find will be in aid of government policy.

(16) To indemnify directors, officers, employees, and agents of the corporation and to purchase and maintain liability insurance for those persons as, and to the extent, permitted by Article 2.02-1 of this Act.

(17) To pay pensions and establish pension plans, pension trusts, profit sharing plans, stock bonus plans, and other incentive plans for all of, or

class, or classes of its officers and employees, or its officers or its employees.

(18) To be an organizer, partner, member, associate, or manager of any partnership, joint venture, or other enterprise, and to the extent permitted in any other jurisdiction to be an incorporator of any other corporation of any type or kind.

(19) To cease its corporate activities and terminate its existence by voluntary dissolution.

(20) Whether included in the foregoing or not, to have and exercise all powers necessary or appropriate to effect any or all of the purposes for which the corporation is organized.

(Section 2.02-1 not reproduced.)

B. Nothing in this Article grants any authority to officers or directors of a corporation for the exercise of any of the foregoing powers, inconsistent with limitations on any of the same which may be expressly set forth in this Act or in the articles of incorporation or in any other laws of this state. Authority of officers and directors to act beyond the scope of the purpose or purposes of a corporation is not granted by any provision of this Article.

C. Nothing contained in this Article shall be deemed to authorize any action in violation of the Anti-Trust Laws of this state or of any of the provisions of Part Four of the Texas Miscellaneous Corporation Laws Act, as now existing or hereafter amended.

Art. 2.28. Quorum of Shareholders

A. Unless otherwise provided in the articles of incorporation, the holders of a majority of the shares entitled to

vote, represented in person or by proxy, shall constitute a quorum at a meeting of shareholders, but in no
event shall a quorum consist of the holders of less than
one-third ($^{1}/_{3}$) of the shares entitled to vote and thus
represented at such meeting. The vote of the holders of
a majority of the shares entitled to vote and thus represented at a meeting at which a quorum is present shall
be the act of the shareholders' meeting, unless the vote
of a greater number is required by law, the articles of
incorporation or bylaws.

Art. 2.29. Voting of Shares

A. (1) Each outstanding share, regardless of class, shall
be entitled to one vote on each matter submitted to
a vote at a meeting of shareholders, except:
(a) To the extent that the articles of incorporation
provide for more or less than one vote per
share or (if and to the extent permitted by this
Act) limit or deny voting rights to the holders
of the shares of any class or series, or
(b) As otherwise provided by this Act.
(2) If the articles of incorporation provide for more or
less than one vote per share for all the outstanding
shares or for the shares of any class or any series
on any matter, every reference in this Act (or in
the articles of incorporation or bylaws, unless expressly stated otherwise therein), in connection
with such matter, to a specified portion of such
shares shall mean such portion of the votes entitled to be cast in respect of such shares by virtue
of the provisions of such articles of incorporation.
B. Treasury shares, shares of its own stock owned by another corporation the majority of the voting stock of

which is owned or controlled by it, and shares of its own stock held by a corporation in a fiduciary capacity shall not be voted, directly or indirectly, at any meeting, and shall not be counted in determining the total number of outstanding shares at any given time.

C. A shareholder may vote either in person or by proxy executed in writing by the shareholder or by his duly authorized attorney in fact. No proxy shall be valid after eleven (11) months from the date of its execution unless otherwise provided in the proxy. A proxy shall be revocable unless expressly provided therein to be irrevocable and unless otherwise made irrevocable by law.

D. (1) At each election for directors every shareholder entitled to vote at such election shall have the right to vote, in person or by proxy, the number of shares owned by him for as many persons as there are directors to be elected and for whose election he has a right to vote, or unless expressly prohibited by the articles of incorporation to cumulate his votes by giving one candidate as many votes as the number of such directors multiplied by his shares shall equal, or by distributing such votes on the same principle among any number of such candidates.

(2) Any shareholder who intends to cumulate his votes as herein authorized shall give written notice of such intention to the secretary of the corporation on or before the day preceding the election at which such shareholder intends to cumulate his votes. All shareholders may cumulate their votes if any shareholder gives the written notice provided for herein.

E. Shares standing in the name of another corporation, domestic or foreign, may be voted by such officer, agent, or proxy as the bylaws of such corporation may authorize or, in the absence of such authorization, as the board of directors of such corporation may determine; provided, however, that when any foreign corporation without a permit to do business in this state lawfully owns or may lawfully own or acquire stock in Texas corporation, it shall not be unlawful for such foreign corporation to vote said stock and participate in the management and control of the business and affairs of such Texas corporation, as other stockholders, subject to all laws, rules, and regulations governing Texas corporations and especially subject to the provisions of the Anti-Trust laws of the state of Texas.

F. Shares held by an administrator, executor, guardian, or conservator may be voted by him so long as such shares forming a part of an estate are in the possession and forming a part of the estate being served by him, either in person or by proxy, without a transfer of such shares into his name. Shares standing in the name of a trustee may be voted by him, either in person or by proxy, but no trustee shall be entitled to vote shares held by him without a transfer of such shares into his name as trustee.

G. Shares standing in the name of a receiver may be voted by such a receiver, and shares held by or under the control of a receiver may be voted by such receiver without the transfer thereof into his name if authority so to do be contained in an appropriate order of the court by which such receiver was appointed.

H. A shareholder whose shares are pledged shall be entitled to vote such shares until the shares have been transferred into the name of the pledgee, and thereafter the pledgee shall be entitled to vote the shares so transferred.

Art. 2.32. Number and Election of Directors

A. The board of directors of a corporation shall consist of one or more members. The number of directors shall be fixed by, or in the manner provided in, the articles of incorporation or the bylaws, except as to the number constituting the initial board of directors, which number shall be fixed by the articles of incorporation. The number of directors may be increased or decreased from time to time by amendment to or in the manner provided in, the articles of incorporation or the bylaws, but no decrease shall have the effect of shortening the term of any incumbent director. In the absence of a bylaw providing for the number of directors, the number shall be the same as that provided for in the articles of incorporation. The names and addresses of the members of the initial board of directors shall be stated in the articles of incorporation. Unless removed in accordance with the provisions of the bylaws or the articles of incorporation, such persons shall hold office until the first annual meeting of shareholders, and until their successors shall have been elected and qualified. At the first annual meeting of shareholders and at each annual meeting thereafter the shareholders shall elect directors to hold office until the next succeeding annual meeting, except in case of the classification of directors as permitted by this Act. Unless removed in accordance with provisions of the bylaws or the articles of incorporation, each director shall hold office for the term for which he is elected and until his successor shall have been elected and qualified. The bylaws or the articles of incorporation may provide that at any meeting of shareholders called expressly for that purpose any director or the

entire board of directors may be removed, with or
without cause, by a vote of the holders of a majority of
the shares then entitled to vote at an election of directors, subject to any further restrictions on removal
which may be contained in the bylaws. In the case of a
corporation having cumulative voting, if less than the
entire board is to be removed, no one of the directors
may be removed if the votes cast against his removal
would be sufficient to elect him if then cumulatively
voted at an election of the entire board of directors, or
if there be classes of directors, at an election of the
class of directors of which he is a part.

Art. 2.35. Quorum of Directors

A. A majority of the number of directors fixed by, or in
    the manner provided in, the articles of incorporation
    or the bylaws shall constitute a quorum for the trans-
    action of business unless a greater number is required
    by law or the articles of incorporation or the bylaws.
    The act of the majority of the directors present at a
    meeting at which a quorum is present shall be the act
    of the board of directors, unless the act of a greater
    number is required by law or the articles of incorpora-
    tion or the bylaws.

Art. 2.41. Liability of Directors and Shareholders in Certain Cases

A. In addition to any other liabilities imposed by law upon
    directors of a corporation:
    (1) Directors of a corporation who vote for or assent
        to the declaration of any dividend or other distri-

bution of the assets of a corporation to its shareholders that, on the date of that vote or assent, violates the provisions of this Act, or any restrictions contained in the articles of incorporation, shall be jointly and severally liable to the corporation for the amount of such dividend which is paid, or the value of such assets which are distributed in excess of the amount of such dividends or distribution which could have been paid or distributed without violating the provisions of this Act or the restrictions in the articles of incorporation.

(2) Directors of a corporation who vote for or assent to a purchase of its own shares that, on the date of that vote or assent, violates the provisions of this Act shall be jointly and severally liable to the corporation for the amount of consideration paid for such shares which is in excess of the maximum amount which could have been paid therefor without violating the provisions of this Act.

(3) The directors of a corporation who vote for or assent to any distribution of assets of a corporation to its shareholders during the liquidation of the corporation without the payment and discharge of, or making adequate provision for, all debts, obligations, and liabilities of the corporation known to the directors on the date of that vote or assent shall be jointly and severally liable to the corporation for the value of such assets which are distributed, to the extent that such debts, obligations, and liabilities of the corporation are not thereafter paid and discharged.

(4) The directors of a corporation who vote for or assent to the making of a loan to an officer or director of the corporation in violation of this Act shall be jointly and severally liable to the corporation

for the amount of such loan until the repayment thereof.

(5) If the corporation shall commence business before it has received for the issuance of shares consideration of the value of at least One Thousand Dollars ($1,000), consisting of money, labor done, or property actually received, the directors who assent thereto shall be jointly and severally liable to the corporation for such part of the required consideration as shall not have been received before commencing business, but such liability shall be terminated when the corporation has actually received the required consideration for the issuance of shares.

(6) In the event of the insolvency of a corporation, directors who have voted for or assented to any payments out of the reduction surplus of the corporation, whether in the course of a distribution in partial liquidation or as the purchase price of shares issued by the corporation and later purchased by it, shall be liable to the corporation, or to its receiver or trustee in bankruptcy, to the extent of the amount of such payments made, for the purpose of discharging creditor claims against the corporation which existed at the time such payments were made or which were incurred within thirty (30) days after notice of the reduction of stated capital had been filed, but such liability shall be imposed only to the extent that such creditor claims have not been fully paid after such creditors have shared with other creditors in the assets of the corporation. Any director against whom a claim shall be asserted under this subsection, and who shall be held liable thereon, shall be entitled to contribution from the shareholders who ac-

cepted or received such payments out of reduction surplus, to the extent of the amounts of such payments received by them, respectively.

B. A director of a corporation who is present at a meeting of its board of directors at which action on any corporate matter is taken shall be presumed to have assented to the action taken unless his dissent shall be entered in the minutes of the meeting or unless he shall file his written dissent to such action with the person acting as the secretary of the meeting before the adjournment thereof or shall forward such dissent by registered mail to the secretary of the corporation immediately after the adjournment of the meeting. Such right to dissent shall not apply to a director who voted in favor of such action.

C. A director shall not be liable under subsections (1), (2), or (3) of Section A of this Article, if, in the exercise of ordinary care, he relied and acted in good faith upon financial statements or other information of the corporation represented to him to be correct in all material respects by the president or by the officer of such corporation having charge of its books of account, or reported by an independent public or certified public accountant or firm of such accountants to present fairly the financial position of such corporation, nor shall he be so liable if, in the exercise of ordinary care and in good faith, in determining the amount available for any such dividend or distribution, he considered the assets to be of their book value.

D. A director shall not be liable for any claims or damages that may result from his acts in the discharge of any duty imposed or power conferred upon him by the corporation if, in the exercise of ordinary care, he acted in good faith and in reliance upon the written opinion of an attorney for the corporation.

E. A director against whom a claim shall be asserted under this Article for the payment of a dividend or other distribution of assets of a corporation, and who shall be held liable thereon, shall be entitled to contribution from the shareholders who accepted or received such dividend or assets knowing such dividend or distribution to have been made in violation of this Article, in proportion to the amounts received by them, respectively.

F. A director against whom a claim shall be asserted under this Article shall be entitled to contribution from the other directors who voted for or assented to the action upon which the claim is asserted.

Art. 2.44. Books and Records

A. Each corporation shall keep correct and complete books and records of account and shall keep minutes of the proceedings of its shareholders and board of directors and shall keep at its registered office or principal place of business, or at the office of its transfer agent or registrar, a record of its shareholders, giving the names and addresses of all shareholders and the number and class of the shares held by each. Any books, records, and minutes may be in written form or in any other form capable of being converted into written form within a reasonable time.

B. Any person who shall have been a holder of record of shares for at least six (6) months immediately preceding his demand, or shall be the holder of record of at least five percent (5%) of all the outstanding shares of a corporation, upon written demand stating the purpose thereof, shall have the right to examine, in person or by agent, accountant, or attorney, at any reasonable time or times, for any proper purpose, its relevant books and records of account, minutes, and record of shareholders, and to make extracts therefrom.

C. Any corporation which shall refuse to allow any such shareholder or his agent, accountant, or attorney to examine and make extracts from its books and records of account, minutes, and record of shareholders, for any proper purpose, shall be liable to such shareholder for all costs and expenses, including attorneys' fees, incurred in enforcing his rights under this Article in addition to any other damages or remedy afforded him by law. It shall be a defense to any action for penalties under this section that the person suing therefor has within two (2) years sold or offered for sale any list of shareholders or of holders of voting trust certificates for shares of such corporation or any other corporation or has aided or abetted any person in procuring any list of shareholders or of holders of voting trust certificates for any such purpose, or has improperly used any information secured through any prior examination of the books and records of account, or minutes, or record of shareholders or of holders of voting trust certificates for shares of such corporation or any other corporation, or was not acting in good faith or for a proper purpose in making his demand.

D. Nothing herein contained shall impair the power of any court of competent jurisdiction, upon proof of proper purpose by a beneficial or record holder of shares, irrespective of the period of time during which such holder shall have been a beneficial or record holder and irrespective of the number of shares held by him, to compel the production for examination by such holder of the books and records of account, minutes, and record of shareholders of a corporation.

E. Upon the written request of any holder of record of shares of a corporation, the corporation shall mail to such holder its annual statements for its last fiscal year showing in reasonable detail its assets and liabilities and the results of its operations and the most recent interim statements, if any, which have been filed in a public record or otherwise published. The corporation shall be allowed a reasonable time to prepare such annual statements.

F. A holder of a beneficial interest in a voting trust complying with this Act shall be regarded as a holder of record of shares with respect to the shares represented by such beneficial interest for the purposes of this Article.

Glossary

Annual Meeting—The yearly meeting of the shareholders and directors of a corporation at which new directors and officers are elected, and a review is made of the past year's corporate business.

Articles of Incorporation—The document containing preliminary information about the corporation that is submitted to the secretary of state of Texas requesting that a corporation be chartered and created.

Assets—An accounting term describing the property owned by the corporation that has a value to the corporation.

Assumed Name Certificate—A document filed with the county clerk of the county in which a business is located naming the individuals that own a company being operated under a name other than the individual's name.

Audit—A review by an accountant of the financial records of a corporation for the purpose of expressing an opinion on the fairness of that firm's financial statements.

Balance Sheet—A report showing the assets, liabilities, and capital of a business as of a certain date.

Board of Directors—A group of individuals elected by the shareholders of a corporation and responsible for the management of the business and affairs of the corporation.

Buy-Sell Agreement—Also known as a stock purchase agreement, this agreement provides for the transfer of stock to the corporation or the other shareholders in the event of the death, withdrawal, or retirement of a shareholder.

Bylaws—The basic rules for the operation of the corporation, adopted by the board of directors of the corporation.

Capital—Also known as shareholder's equity, this reflects the ownership claim on the assets of a corporation by its shareholders.

Capital Gains—A form of financial gain upon the sale of capital assets, including stock in a corporation, which may receive a very favorable tax treatment.

Capital Stock—The form of ownership of a corporation resulting from the sale of shares of stock to shareholders.

Cash Flow—The inflow and outflow of cash in a corporation.

Certificate of Incorporation—A document issued by the secretary of state of Texas reflecting the existence of a corporation.

Certified Public Accountant—An accountant licensed to practice as an accountant having met the educational, testing, and experience requirements set by the state of Texas.

Close Corporation—A term normally used to denote a small corporation with few shareholders. It may also be used in reference to a corporation formed under the Texas Closed Corporation Act.

Contract—A legal agreement between two or more parties setting forth certain rights and obligations of each party.

Corporation Book—A book containing the legal documents, including the minutes, bylaws, and certificate of incorporation relative to the formation and operation of the corporation.

Corporate Seal—A small mechanical device that will place on documents an impression containing the corporation's name.

Corporate Tax Rate—The rate of income tax as is applied to a corporation.

Corporation—A business that has become incorporated under the laws of the state of Texas or another state.

Creditors—Those individuals or other businesses to whom money is owed.

Debts—An obligation to pay a sum of money to a certain individual or company.

Dividends—A distribution of cash or stock by a corporation to its shareholders.

Expenses—The cost of goods or services used in the operation of a business.

Earned Surplus—An obsolete term for retained earnings.

Federal Corporate Income Tax Return—Form 1120, the income tax return filed by a corporation.

Securities and Exchange Commission—The government agency that regulates the sale of corporate stock to the public.

F.I.C.A. Tax—The Federal Insurance Contributions Act, the tax on employees and employers for social security and related benefits.

Financial Statements—The accounting reports that reflect the financial standing of a business. The routine statements for a corporation are the income statement, the balance sheet, and the statement of retained earnings. Also prepared may be a fourth statement, the statement of changes in financial position.

Fiscal Year—A one-year period that may be the calendar year or any other twelve-month period.

Form 1040—The form filed by an individual to report his personal income and the tax thereon.

Form 1065—The form filed by a partnership to report its income.

Form 2553—The form filed by a corporation in its election to become a subchapter S corporation and be taxed as a partnership.

Form SS-4—The form used to apply for an employer's identification number with the Internal Revenue Service.

Franchise Tax—The annual tax charged by the state of Texas to Texas corporations for the privilege of holding a corporate charter.

Fringe Benefits—Benefits of a personal nature that would otherwise have to be paid for by an individual, but are furnished to him free of charge by virtue of his employment with a corporation.

General Journal—An accounting book in which to record in a uniform manner business transactions of the company.

General Ledger—An accounting book containing all accounts of the business and in which is stored accounting information for the business.

General Purpose Clause—A purpose clause used in the articles of incorporation allowing the business to engage in any business activity in which a duly organized corporation may engage.

Incorporate—To create a corporation for a new or existing business.

Incorporators—Those individuals, whether one or more, that have incorporated a new or existing business.

Liability—As a legal term, it means the responsibility for a certain action or event is determined to be that of a certain party. As an accounting term, it means that a debt or obligation is owed to a certain party.

Limited Partnership—A form of partnership having general partners who manage the business and have unlimited liability therefor, and limited partners who have no management authority and limited liability for business debts.

Limited Liability—When used in reference to a corporation, it means that a shareholder's maximum loss in the event that the corporation is sued is the amount of his investment in the corporation.

Medical Reimbursement Plan—A plan adopted by a corporation allowing it to reimburse employees for their medical expenses.

Minutes—A written record of the activities having occurred at a corporate meeting.

Net Income—The amount by which the revenues of a business exceed the expenses of operating the business.

Nonprofit Corporation—A corporation formed for some purpose other than making a profit for its shareholders.

Officers—Those individuals elected by the board of directors of a corporation responsible for the daily operation of the corporation.

One-Write System—Also known as a peg board system, this is a commercially available accounting system where one action, such as writing a check, will perform several accounting transactions at one time.

Ordinary Gains Basis—A financial gain taxed at an individual's regular tax rate.

Organizational meeting—The initial meeting of the organizers of the corporation at which the board of directors and officers are elected and formative matters are decided upon.

Partnership—Two or more individuals joined together to engage in a business for profit.

Pierce the Corporate Veil—A legal term meaning that a corporation has lost its characteristic of limited liability, usually as a result of noncompliance with the corporate formalities of doing business.

Professional Association—A corporate form of doing business used by licensed physicians.

Professional Corporation—A corporate form of doing business used by licensed professionals including but not limited to accountants, attorneys, and veterinarians.

Profit—A term used by many individuals to denote the net income of the business.

Promissory Note—A written document describing a debt and its terms, signed by the debtor.

Quorum—The required number of individuals, usually officers or directors, that when present are authorized to conduct business for the corporation.

Retirement Plan—Generally, a systematic setting aside of corporate funds to provide for the retirement of corporate employees.

Reservation of Corporate Name—The legal process of reserving a selected corporate name for a period of 120 days, during which time no other individual may incorporate under such name.

Resolution—A statement of intent on a certain matter, considered, voted upon and adopted by the corporation officers or directors, and formally documented in the minutes of the corporation.

Retained Earnings—The earnings of a corporation that have been retained within the business and not paid out to shareholders as dividends. Still referred to as earned surplus by many attorneys.

Revenue—The overall receipts of the business prior to the deduction of expenses.

Registered Agent—The individual to whom, as a representative of the corporation, communications, legal or otherwise, may be directed.

Schedule C—That portion of an individual's Form 1040 where the revenue, expenses, and resulting profits or losses are detailed.

Secretary of State of Texas—The elected official whose duties, among many others, are to regulate the creation and existence of corporations in Texas.

Sole Proprietorship—One individual engaging in a business for profit.

Special Meeting—A corporate meeting, other than a regularly scheduled meeting, called to conduct some special business for the corporation.

Stock Certificate—The printed certificate that reflects the ownership of shares of stock in a corporation.

Stockholder—A person who has an ownership interest, either in whole or in part, of a corporation.

Stockholder's Ledger—The official corporate record of the individuals who own stock in the corporation, usually including their address, number of shares held, and the amount paid to the corporation for their shares.

Subchapter S Corporation—A corporation that has elected under the Internal Revenue Code to be taxed on its income as a partnership rather than a corporation.

Tax Planning—The development of a plan for the corporation and its shareholders that will result in the minimum amount of income tax having to be paid on the earnings of the corporation or its distributions to shareholders.

Texas Business Corporation Act—The Texas Statutes that govern the creation and operation of corporations in Texas.

Texas Comptroller—The official whose office, among other duties, collects franchise tax on Texas corporations.

Texas Homestead Act—The act that protects certain property, both land and personal property, from being forcefully sold to satisfy a lawsuit judgement against the owner of the property.

Texas Securities Commission—The State of Texas agency that regulates the public sale of stock to citizens of Texas.

Waiver of Notice—A written permission given by a shareholder or director to conduct a corporate meeting without written notice of the meeting having been previously given to the shareholder or director as required by statute.

Withholding Tax—That portion of an employee's earnings withheld by the employer for the employee's federal income tax and social security tax.

Index